Milan

and

Mantua

Jacques Casanova de Seingalt

[ZHINGOORA BOOKS]

MILAN AND MANTUA

CHAPTER XX

Slight Misfortunes Compel Me to Leave Venice—My Adventures in Milan and Mantua

On Low Sunday Charles paid us a visit with his lovely wife, who seemed totally indifferent to what Christine used to be. Her hair dressed with powder did not please me as well as the raven black of her beautiful locks, and her fashionable town attire did not, in my eyes, suit her as well as her rich country dress. But the countenances of husband and wife bore the stamp of happiness. Charles reproached me in a friendly manner because I had not called once upon them, and, in order to atone for my apparent negligence, I went to see them the next day with M. Dandolo. Charles told me that his wife was idolized by his aunt and his sister who had become her bosom friend; that she was kind, affectionate, unassuming, and of a disposition which enforced affection. I was no less pleased with this favourable state of things than with the facility with which Christine was learning the Venetian dialect.

When M. Dandolo and I called at their house, Charles was not at home; Christine was alone with his two relatives. The most friendly welcome was proffered to us, and in the course of conversation the aunt praised the progress made by Christine in her writing very highly, and asked her to let me see her copy-book. I followed her to the next room, where she told me that she was very happy; that every day she discovered new virtues in her husband.

He had told her, without the slightest appearance of suspicion of displeasure, that he knew that we had spent two days together in Treviso, and that he had laughed at the well-meaning fool who had given him that piece of information in the hope of raising a cloud in the heaven of their felicity.

Charles was truly endowed with all the virtues, with all the noble qualities of an honest and distinguished man. Twenty-six years afterwards I happened to require the assistance of his purse, and found him my true friend. I never was a frequent visitor at his house, and he appreciated my delicacy. He died a few months before my last departure from Venice, leaving his widow in easy circumstances, and three well-educated sons, all with good positions, who may, for what I know, be still living with their mother.

In June I went to the fair at Padua, and made the acquaintance of a young man of my own age, who was then studying mathematics under the celebrated Professor Succi. His name was Tognolo, but thinking it did not sound well, he changed it for that of Fabris. He became, in after years, Comte de Fabris, lieutenant-general under Joseph II., and died Governor of Transylvania. This man, who owed his high fortune to his talents, would, perhaps, have lived and died unknown if he had kept his name of Tognolo, a truly vulgar one. He was from Uderzo, a large village of the Venetian Friuli. He had a brother in the Church, a man of parts, and a great gamester, who, having a deep knowledge of the world, had taken the name of Fabris, and the younger brother had to assume it likewise. Soon afterwards he bought an estate with the title of count, became a Venetian nobleman, and his origin as a country bumpkin was forgotten. If he had kept his name of Tognolo it would have injured him, for he could not have pronounced it without reminding his hearers of what is called, by the most contemptible of prejudices, low extraction, and the privileged class, through an absurd error, does not admit the possibility of a peasant having talent or genius. No doubt a time will come when society, more enlightened, and therefore more reasonable, will acknowledge that noble feelings, honour, and heroism can be found in every condition of life as easily as in a class, the blood of which is not always exempt from the taint of a misalliance.

The new count, while he allowed others to forget his origin, was too wise to forget it himself, and in legal documents he always signed his family name as well as the one he had adopted. His brother had offered him two ways to win fortune in the world, leaving him perfectly free in his choice. Both required an expenditure of one thousand sequins, but the abbe had put the amount aside for that purpose. My friend had to choose between the sword of Mars and the bird of Minerva. The abbe knew that he could purchase for his brother a company in the army of his Imperial and Apostolic Majesty, or obtain for him a professorship at the University of Padua; for money can do everything. But my friend, who was gifted with noble feelings and good sense, knew that in either profession talents and knowledge were essentials, and before making a choice he was applying himself with great success to the study of mathematics. He ultimately decided upon the military profession, thus imitating Achilles, who preferred the sword to the distaff, and he paid for it with his life like the son of

Peleus; though not so young, and not through a wound inflicted by an arrow, but from the plague, which he caught in the unhappy country in which the indolence of Europe allows the Turks to perpetuate that fearful disease.

The distinguished appearance, the noble sentiments, the great knowledge, and the talents of Fabris would have been turned into ridicule in a man called Tognolo, for such is the force of prejudices, particularly of those which have no ground to rest upon, that an ill-sounding name is degrading in this our stupid society. My opinion is that men who have an ill-sounding name, or one which presents an indecent or ridiculous idea, are right in changing it if they intend to win honour, fame, and fortune either in arts or sciences. No one can reasonably deny them that right, provided the name they assume belongs to nobody. The alphabet is general property, and everyone has the right to use it for the creation of a word forming an appellative sound. But he must truly create it. Voltaire, in spite of his genius, would not perhaps have reached posterity under his name of Arouet, especially amongst the French, who always give way so easily to their keen sense of ridicule and equivocation. How could they have imagined that a writer 'a rouet' could be a man of genius? And D'Alembert, would he have attained his high fame, his universal reputation, if he had been satisfied with his name of M. Le Rond, or Mr. Allround? What would have become of Metastasio under his true name of Trapasso? What impression would Melanchthon have made with his name of Schwarzerd? Would he then have dared to raise the voice of a moralist philosopher, of a reformer of the Eucharist, and so many other holy things? Would not M. de Beauharnais have caused some persons to laugh and others to blush if he had kept his name of Beauvit, even if the first founder of his family had been indebted for his fortune to the fine quality expressed by that name?

Would the Bourbeux have made as good a figure on the throne as the Bourbons? I think that King Poniatowski ought to have abdicated the name of Augustus, which he had taken at the time of his accession to the throne, when he abdicated royalty. The Coleoni of Bergamo, however, would find it rather difficult to change their name, because they would be compelled at the same time to change their coat of arms (the two generative glands), and thus to annihilate the glory of their ancestor, the hero Bartholomeo.

Towards the end of autumn my friend Fabris introduced me to a family in the midst of which the mind and the heart could find delicious food. That family resided in the country on the road to Zero. Card-playing, lovemaking, and practical jokes were the order of the day. Some of those jokes were rather severe ones, but the order of the day was never to get angry and to laugh at everything, for one was to take every jest pleasantly or be thought a bore. Bedsteads would at night tumble down under their occupants, ghosts were personated, diuretic pills or sugar-plums were given to young ladies, as well as comfits who produced certain winds rising from the netherlands, and impossible to keep under control. These jokes would sometimes go rather too far, but such was the spirit animating all the members of that circle; they would laugh. I was not less inured than the others to the war of offence and defence, but at last there was such a bitter joke played upon me that it suggested to me another, the fatal consequences of which put a stop to the mania by which we were all possessed.

We were in the habit of walking to a farm which was about half a league distant by the road, but the distance could be reduced by half by going over a deep and miry ditch across which a narrow plank was thrown, and I always insisted upon going that way, in spite of the fright of the ladies who always trembled on the narrow bridge, although I never failed to cross the first, and to offer my hand to help them over. One fine day, I crossed first so as to give them courage, but suddenly, when I reached the middle of the plank, it gave way under me, and there I was in the ditch, up to the chin in stinking mud, and, in spite of my inward rage, obliged, according to the general understanding, to join in the merry laughter of all my companions. But the merriment did not last long, for the joke was too bad, and everyone declared it to be so. Some peasants were called to the rescue, and with much difficulty they dragged me out in the most awful state. An entirely new dress, embroidered with spangles, my silk stockings, my lace, everything, was of course spoiled, but not minding it, I laughed more heartily that anybody else, although I had already made an inward vow to have the most cruel revenge. In order to know the author of that bitter joke I had only to appear calm and indifferent about it. It was evident that the plank had been purposely sawn. I was taken back to the house, a shirt, a coat, a complete costume, were lent me, for I had come that time only for twenty-four hours, and had not brought anything with me. I went to the city the next morning, and towards the evening I returned to the gay company. Fabris, who had been as angry as myself, observed to me that the perpetrator of the joke evidently felt his guilt, because he took good care not to discover himself. But I unveiled the mystery by promising one sequin to a peasant woman if she could find out who had sawn the plank. She contrived to discover the young man who had done the work. I called on him, and the offer of a sequin, together with my threats, compelled him to confess that he had been paid for his work by Signor Demetrio, a Greek, dealer in spices, a good and amiable man of between forty-five and fifty years, on whom I never played any trick, except in the case of a pretty, young servant girl whom he was courting, and whom I had juggled from him.

Satisfied with my discovery, I was racking my brain to invent a good practical joke, but to obtain complete revenge it was necessary that my trick should prove worse than the one he had played upon me. Unfortunately my imagination was at bay. I could not find anything. A funeral put an end to my difficulties.

Armed with my hunting-knife, I went alone to the cemetery a little after midnight, and opening the grave of the dead man who had been buried that very day, I cut off one of the arms near the shoulder, not without some trouble, and after I had re-buried the corpse, I returned to my room with the arm of the defunct. The next day, when supper was over, I left the table and retired to my chamber as if I intended to go to bed, but taking the arm with me I hid myself under Demetrio's bed. A short time after, the Greek comes in, undresses himself, put his light out, and lies down. I give him time to fall nearly asleep; then, placing myself at the foot of the bed, I pull away the clothes little by little until he is half naked. He laughs and calls out,

"Whoever you may be, go away and let me sleep quietly, for I do not believe in ghosts;" he covers himself again and composes himself to sleep.

I wait five or six minutes, and pull again at the bedclothes; but when he tries to draw up the sheet, saying that he does not care for ghosts, I oppose some resistance. He sits up so as to catch the hand which is pulling at the clothes, and I take care that he should get hold of the dead hand. Confident that he has caught the man or the woman who was playing the trick, he pulls it towards him, laughing all the time; I keep tight hold of the arm for a few instants, and then let it go suddenly; the Greek falls back on his pillow without uttering a single word.

The trick was played, I leave the room without any noise, and, reaching my chamber, go to bed.

I was fast asleep, when towards morning I was awoke by persons going about, and not understanding why they should be up so early, I got up. The first person I met—the mistress of the house—told me that I had played an abominable joke.

"I? What have I done?"

"M. Demetrio is dying."

"Have I killed him?"

She went away without answering me. I dressed myself, rather frightened, I confess, but determined upon pleading complete ignorance of everything, and I proceeded to Demetrio's room; and I was confronted with horror-stricken countenances and bitter reproaches. I found all the guests around him. I protested my innocence, but everyone smiled. The archpriest and the beadle, who had just arrived, would not bury the arm which was lying there, and they told me that I had been guilty of a great crime.

"I am astonished, reverend sir," I said to the priest, "at the hasty judgment which is thus passed upon me, when there is no proof to condemn me."

"You have done it," exclaimed all the guests, "you alone are capable of such an abomination; it is just like you. No one but you would have dared to do such a thing!"

"I am compelled," said the archpriest, "to draw up an official report."

"As you please, I have not the slightest objection," I answered, "I have nothing to fear."

And I left the room.

I continued to take it coolly, and at the dinner-table I was informed that M. Demetrio had been bled, that he had recovered the use of his eyes, but not of his tongue or of his limbs. The next day he could speak, and I heard, after I had taken leave of the family, that he was stupid and spasmodic. The poor man remained in that painful state for the rest of his life. I felt deeply grieved, but I had not intended to injure him so badly. I thought that the trick he had played upon me might have cost my life, and I could not help deriving consolation from that idea.

On the same day, the archpriest made up his mind to have the arm buried, and to send a formal denunciation against me to the episcopal chancellorship of Treviso.

Annoyed at the reproaches which I received on all sides, I returned to Venice. A fortnight afterwards I was summoned to appear before the 'magistrato alla blasfemia'. I begged M. Barbaro to enquire the cause of the aforesaid summons, for it was a formidable court. I was surprised at the proceedings being taken against me, as if there had been a certainty of my having desecrated a grave, whilst there could be nothing but suspicion. But I was mistaken, the summons was not relating to that affair. M. Barbaro informed me in the evening that a woman had brought a complaint against me for having violated her daughter. She stated in her complaint that, having decoyed her child to the Zuecca, I had abused her by violence, and she adduced as a proof that her daughter was confined to her bed, owing to the bad treatment she had received from me in my endeavours to ravish her. It was one of those complaints which are often made, in order to give trouble and to cause expense, even against innocent persons. I was innocent of violation, but it was quite true that I had given the girl a sound thrashing. I prepared my defence, and begged M. Barbaro to deliver it to the magistrate's secretary.

DECLARATION

I hereby declare that, on such a day, having met the woman with her daughter, I accosted them and offered to give them some refreshments at a coffee-house near by; that the daughter refused to accept my caresses, and that the mother said to me,—

"My daughter is yet a virgin, and she is quite right not to lose her maidenhood without making a good profit by it."

"If so," I answered, "I will give you ten sequins for her virginity."

"You may judge for yourself," said the mother.

Having assured myself of the fact by the assistance of the sense of feeling, and having ascertained that it might be true, I told the mother to bring the girl in the afternoon to the Zuecca, and that I would give her the ten sequins. My offer was joyfully accepted, the mother brought her daughter to me, she received the money, and leaving us together in the Garden of the Cross, she went away. When I tried to avail myself of the right for which I had paid, the girl, most likely trained to the business by her mother, contrived to prevent me. At first the game amused me, but at last, being tired of it, I told her to have done. She answered quietly that it was not her fault if I was not able to do what I wanted. Vexed and annoyed, I placed her in such a position that she found herself at bay, but, making a violent effort, she managed to change her position and debarred me from making any further attempts.

"Why," I said to her, "did you move?"

"Because I would not have it in that position."

"You would not?"

"No."

Without more ado, I got hold of a broomstick, and gave her a good lesson, in order to get something for the ten sequins which I had been foolish enough to pay in advance. But I have broken none of her limbs, and I took care to apply my blows only on her posteriors, on which spot I have no doubt that all the marks may be seen. In the evening I made her dress herself again, and sent her back in a boat which chanced to pass, and she was landed in safety. The mother received ten sequins, the daughter has kept her hateful maidenhood, and, if I am guilty of anything, it is only of having given a thrashing to an infamous girl, the pupil of a still more infamous mother.

My declaration had no effect. The magistrate was acquainted with the girl, and the mother laughed at having duped me so easily. I was summoned, but did not appear before the court, and a writ was on the point of being issued against my body, when the complaint of the profanation of a grave was filed against me before the same magistrate. It would have been less serious for me if the second affair had been carried before the Council of Ten, because one court might have saved me from the other.

The second crime, which, after all, was only a joke, was high felony in the eyes of the clergy, and a great deal was made of it. I was summoned to appear within twenty-four hours, and it was evident that I would be arrested immediately afterwards. M. de Bragadin, who always gave good advice, told me that the best way to avoid the threatening storm was to run away. The advice was certainly wise, and I lost no time in getting ready.

I have never left Venice with so much regret as I did then, for I had some pleasant intrigues on hand, and I was very lucky at cards. My three friends assured me that, within one year at the furthest, the cases against me would be forgotten, and in Venice, when public opinion has forgotten anything, it can be easily arranged.

I left Venice in the evening and the next day I slept at Verona. Two days afterwards I reached Mantua. I was alone, with plenty of clothes and jewels, without letters of introduction, but with a well-filled purse, enjoying excellent health and my twenty-three years.

In Mantua I ordered an excellent dinner, the very first thing one ought to do at a large hotel, and after dinner I went out for a walk. In the evening, after I had seen the coffee-houses and the places of resort, I went to the theatre, and I was delighted to see Marina appear on the stage as a comic dancer, amid the greatest applause, which she deserved, for she danced beautifully. She was tall, handsome, very well made and very graceful. I immediately resolved on renewing my acquaintance with her, if she happened to be free, and after the opera I engaged a boy to take me to her house. She had just sat down to supper with someone, but the moment she saw me she threw her napkin down and flew to my arms. I returned her kisses, judging by her warmth that her guest was a man of no consequence.

The servant, without waiting for orders, had already laid a plate for me, and Marina invited me to sit down near her. I felt vexed, because the aforesaid individual had not risen to salute me, and before I accepted Marina's invitation I asked her who the gentleman was, begging her to introduce me.

"This gentleman," she said, "is Count Celi, of Rome; he is my lover."

"I congratulate you," I said to her, and turning towards the so-called count, "Sir," I added, "do not be angry at our mutual affection, Marina is my daughter."

"She is a prostitute."

"True," said Marina, "and you can believe the count, for he is my procurer."

At those words, the brute threw his knife at her face, but she avoided it by running away. The scoundrel followed her, but I drew my sword, and said,

"Stop, or you are a dead man."

I immediately asked Marina to order her servant to light me out, but she hastily put a cloak on, and taking my arm she entreated me to take her with me.

"With pleasure," I said.

The count then invited me to meet him alone, on the following day, at the
Casino of Pomi, to hear what he had to say.

"Very well, sir, at four in the afternoon," I answered.

I took Marina to my inn, where I lodged her in the room adjoining mine, and we sat down to supper.

Marina, seeing that I was thoughtful, said,

"Are you sorry to have saved me from the rage of that brute?"

"No, I am glad to have done so, but tell me truly who and what he is."

"He is a gambler by profession, and gives himself out as Count Celi. I made his acquaintance here. He courted me, invited me to supper, played after supper, and, having won a large sum from an Englishman whom he had decoyed to his supper by telling him that I would be present, he gave me fifty guineas, saying that he had given me an interest in his bank. As soon as I had become his mistress, he insisted upon my being compliant with all the men he wanted to make his dupes, and at last he took up his quarters at my lodgings. The welcome I gave you very likely vexed him, and you know the rest. Here I am, and here I will remain until my departure for Mantua where I have an engagement as first dancer. My servant will bring me all I need for to-night, and I will give him orders to move all my luggage to-morrow. I will not see that scoundrel any more. I will be only yours, if you are free as in Corfu, and if you love me still."

"Yes, my dear Marina, I do love you, but if you wish to be my mistress, you must be only mine."

"Oh! of course. I have three hundred sequins, and I will give them to you to-morrow if you will take me as your mistress."

"I do not want any money; all I want is yourself. Well, it is all arranged; to-morrow evening we shall feel more comfortable."

"Perhaps you are thinking of a duel for to-morrow? But do not imagine such a thing, dearest. I know that man; he is an arrant coward."

"I must keep my engagement with him."

"I know that, but he will not keep his, and I am very glad of it."

Changing the conversation and speaking of our old acquaintances, she informed me that she had quarreled with her brother Petronio, that her sister was primadonna in Genoa, and that Bellino Therese was still in Naples, where she continued to ruin dukes. She concluded by saying;

"I am the most unhappy of the family."

"How so? You are beautiful, and you have become an excellent dancer. Do not be so prodigal of your favours, and you cannot fail to meet with a man who will take care of your fortune."

"To be sparing of my favours is very difficult; when I love, I am no longer mine, but when I do not love, I cannot be amiable. Well, dearest, I could be very happy with you."

"Dear Marina, I am not wealthy, and my honour would not allow me...."

"Hold your tongue; I understand you."

"Why have you not a lady's maid with you instead of a male servant?"

"You are right. A maid would look more respectable, but my servant is so clever and so faithful!"

"I can guess all his qualities, but he is not a fit servant for you."

The next day after dinner I left Marina getting ready for the theatre, and having put everything of value I possessed in my pocket, I took a carriage and proceeded to the Casino of Pomi. I felt confident of disabling the false count, and sent the carriage away. I was conscious of being guilty of great folly in exposing my life with such an adversary. I might have broken my engagement with him without implicating my honour, but, the fact is that I felt well disposed for a fight, and as I was certainly in the right I thought the prospect of a duel very delightful. A visit to a dancer, a brute professing to be a nobleman, who insults her in my presence, who wants to kill her, who allows her to be carried off in his very teeth, and whose only opposition is to give me an appointment! It seemed to me that if I had failed to come, I should have given him the right to call me a coward.

The count had not yet arrived. I entered the coffee-room to wait for him. I met a good-looking Frenchman there, and I addressed him. Being pleased with his conversation, I told him that I expected the arrival of a man, and that as my honour required that he should find me alone I would feel grateful if he would go away as soon as I saw the man approaching. A short time afterwards I saw my adversary coming along, but with a second. I then told the

Frenchman that he would oblige me by remaining, and he accepted as readily as if I had invited him to a party of pleasure. The count came in with his follower, who was sporting a sword at least forty inches long, and had all the look of a cut-throat. I advanced towards the count, and said to him dryly,—

"You told me that you would come alone."

"My friend will not be in the way, as I only want to speak to you."

"If I had known that, I would not have gone out of my way. But do not let us be noisy, and let us go to some place where we can exchange a few words without being seen. Follow me."

I left the coffee-room with the young Frenchman, who, being well acquainted with the place, took me to the most favourable spot, and we waited there for the two other champions, who were walking slowly and talking together. When they were within ten paces I drew my sword and called upon my adversary to get ready. My Frenchman had already taken out his sword, but he kept it under his arm.

"Two to one!" exclaimed Celi.

"Send your friend away, and this gentleman will go likewise; at all events, your friend wears a sword, therefore we are two against two."

"Yes," said the Frenchman, "let us have a four-handed game."

"I do not cross swords with a dancer," said the cutthroat.

He had scarcely uttered those words when my friend, going up to him, told him that a dancer was certainly as good as a blackleg, and gave him a violent bow with the flat of his sword on the face. I followed his example with Celi, who began to beat a retreat, and said that he only wanted to tell me something, and that he would fight afterwards.

"Well, speak."

"You know me and I do not know you. Tell me who you are."

My only answer was to resume laying my sword upon the scoundrel, while the Frenchman was shewing the same dexterity upon the back of his companion, but the two cowards took to their heels, and there was nothing for us to do but to sheathe our weapons. Thus did the duel end in a manner even more amusing than Marina herself had anticipated.

My brave Frenchman was expecting someone at the casino. I left him after inviting him to supper for that evening after the opera. I gave him; the name which I had assumed for my journey and the address of my hotel.

I gave Marina a full description of the adventure.

"I will," she said, "amuse everybody at the theatre this evening with the story of your meeting. But that which pleases me most is that, if your second is really a dancer, he can be no other than M. Baletti, who is engaged with me for the Mantua Theatre."

I stored all my valuables in my trunk again, and went to the opera, where I saw Baletti, who recognized me, and pointed me out to all his friends, to whom he was relating the adventure. He joined me after the performance, and accompanied me to the inn. Marina, who had already returned, came to my room as soon as she heard my voice, and I was amused at the surprise of the amiable Frenchman, when he saw the young artist with whom he had engaged to dance the comic parts. Marina, although an excellent dancer, did not like the serious style. Those two handsome adepts of Terpsichore had never met before, and they began an amorous warfare which made me enjoy my supper immensely, because, as he was a fellow artist, Marina assumed towards Baletti a tone well adapted to the circumstances, and very different to her usual manner with other men. She shone with wit and beauty that evening, and was in an excellent temper, for she had been much applauded by the public, the true version of the Celi business being already well known.

The theatre was to be open only for ten more nights, and as Marina wished to leave Milan immediately after the last performance, we decided on travelling together. In the mean time, I invited Baletti (it was an Italian name which he had adopted for the stage) to be our guest during the remainder of our stay in Milan. The friendship between us had a great influence upon all the subsequent events of my life, as the reader will see in these Memoirs. He had great talent as a dancer, but that was the least of his excellent qualities. He was honest, his feelings were noble, he had studied much, and he had received the best education that could be given in those days in France to a nobleman.

On the third day I saw plainly that Marina wished to make a conquest of her colleague, and feeling what great advantage might accrue to her from it I resolved on helping her. She had a post-chaise for two persons, and I easily persuaded her to take Baletti with her, saying that I wished to arrive alone in Mantua for several reasons which I could not confide to her. The fact was that if I had arrived with her, people would have naturally supposed that I was her lover, and I wished to avoid that. Baletti was delighted with the proposal; he insisted upon paying his share of the expenses, but Marina would not hear of it. The reasons alleged by the young man for paying his own expenses were excellent ones, and it was with great difficulty that I prevailed upon him to accept Marina's offer, but I ultimately succeeded. I promised to wait for them on the road, so as to take dinner and supper together, and on the day appointed for our departure I left Milan one hour before them.

Reaching the city of Cremona very early, where we intended to sleep, I took a walk about the streets, and, finding a coffee-house, I went in. I made there the acquaintance of a French officer, and we left the coffee-room together to take a short ramble. A very pretty woman happened to pass in a carriage, and my companion stopped her to say a few words. Their conversation was soon over, and the officer joined me again.

"Who is that lovely lady?" I enquired.

"She is a truly charming woman, and I can tell you an anecdote about her worthy of being transmitted to posterity. You need not suppose that I am going to exaggerate, for the adventure is known to everybody in Cremona. The charming woman whom you have just seen is gifted with wit greater even than her beauty, and here is a specimen of it. A young officer, one amongst many military men who were courting her, when Marshal de Richelieu was commanding in Genoa, boasted of being treated by her with more favour than all the others, and one day, in the very coffee-room where we met, he advised a brother officer not to lose his time in courting her, because he had no chance whatever of obtaining any favour.

"My dear fellow,' said the other officer, 'I have a much better right to give you that piece of advice; for I have already obtained from her everything which can be granted to a lover.'

"'I am certain that you are telling a lie,' exclaimed the young man, 'and
I request you to follow me out.'

"'Most willingly,' said the indiscreet swain, 'but what is the good of ascertaining the truth through a duel and of cutting our throats, when I can make the lady herself certify the fact in your presence.'

"'I bet twenty-five louis that it is all untrue,' said the incredulous officer.

"'I accept your bet. Let us go.'

"The two contending parties proceeded together towards the dwelling of the lady whom you saw just now, who was to name the winner of the twenty-five louis.

"They found her in her dressing-room. 'Well gentlemen,' she said, 'what lucky wind has brought you here together at this hour?

"'It is a bet, madam,' answered the unbelieving officer, 'and you alone can be the umpire in our quarrel. This gentleman has been boasting of having obtained from you everything a woman can grant to the most favoured lover. I have given him the lie in the most impressive manner, and a duel was to ensue, when he offered to have the truth of his boast certified by you. I have bet twenty-five Louis that you would not admit it, and he has taken my bet. Now, madam, you can say which of us two is right.'

"You have lost, sir," she said to him; 'but now I beg both of you to quit my house, and I give you fair warning that if you ever dare to shew your faces here again, you will be sorry for it.'

"The two heedless fellows went away dreadfully mortified. The unbeliever paid the bet, but he was deeply vexed, called the other a coxcomb, and a week afterwards killed him in a duel.

"Since that time the lady goes to the casino, and continues to mix in society, but does not see company at her own house, and lives in perfect accord with her husband."

"How did the husband take it all?"

"Quite well, and like an intelligent, sensible man. He said that, if his wife had acted differently, he would have applied for a divorce, because in that case no one would have entertained a doubt of her being guilty."

"That husband is indeed a sensible fellow. It is certain that, if his wife had given the lie to the indiscreet officer, he would have paid the bet, but he would have stood by what he had said, and everybody would have believed him. By declaring him the winner of the bet she has cut the matter short, and she has avoided a judgment by which she would have been dishonoured. The inconsiderate boaster was guilty of a double mistake for which he paid the penalty of his life, but his adversary was as much wanting in delicacy, for in such matters rightly-minded men do not venture upon betting. If the one who says yes is imprudent, the one who says no is a dupe. I like the lady's presence of mind."

"But what sentence would you pass on her. Guilty or not guilty?"

"Not guilty."

"I am of the same opinion, and it has been the verdict of the public likewise, for she has since been treated even better than before the affair. You will see, if you go to the casino, and I shall be happy to introduce you to her."

I invited the officer to sup with us, and we spent a very pleasant evening. After he had gone, I remarked with pleasure that Marina was capable of observing the rules of propriety. She had taken a bedroom to herself, so as not to hurt the feelings of her respectable fellow-dancer.

When I arrived in Mantua, I put up at St. Mark's hotel. Marina, to whom I had given a notice that my intention was to call on her but seldom, took up her abode in the house assigned to her by the theatrical manager.

In the afternoon of the same day, as I was walking about, I went into a bookseller's shop to ascertain whether there was any new work out. I remained there without perceiving that the night had come, and on being told that the shop was going to be closed, I went out. I had only gone a few yards when I was arrested by a patrol, the officer of which told me that, as I had no lantern and as eight o'clock had struck, his duty was to take me to the guardhouse. It was in vain that I observed that, having arrived only in the afternoon, I could not know that order of the police. I was compelled to follow him.

When we reached the guardhouse, the officer of the patrol introduced me to his captain, a tall, fine-looking young man who received me in the most cheerful manner. I begged him to let me return to my hotel as I needed rest after my journey. He laughed and answered, "No, indeed, I want you to spend a joyous night with me, and in good company." He told the officer to give me back my sword, and, addressing me again, he said, "I only consider you, my dear sir, as my friend and guest."

I could not help being amused at such a novel mode of invitation, and I accepted it. He gave some orders to a German soldier, and soon afterwards the table was laid out for four persons. The two other officers joined us, and we had a very gay supper. When the desert had been served the company was increased by the arrival of two disgusting, dissolute females. A green cloth was spread over the table, and one of the officers began a faro bank. I punted so as not to appear unwilling to join the game, and after losing a few sequins I went out to breathe the fresh air, for we had drunk freely. One of the two females followed me, teased me, and finally contrived, in spite of myself, to make me a present which condemned me to a regimen of six weeks. After that fine exploit, I went in again.

A young and pleasant officer, who had lost some fifteen or twenty sequins, was swearing like a trooper because the banker had pocketed his money and was going. The young officer had a great deal of gold before him on the table, and he contended that the banker ought to have warned him that it would be the last game.

"Sir," I said to him, politely, "you are in the wrong, for faro is the freest of games. Why do you not take the bank yourself?"

"It would be too much trouble, and these gentlemen do not punt high enough for me, but if that sort of thing amuses you, take the bank and I will punt."

"Captain," I said, "will you take a fourth share in my bank?"

"Willingly."

"Gentlemen, I beg you to give notice that I will lay the cards down after six games."

I asked for new packs of cards, and put three hundred sequins on the table. The captain wrote on the back of a card, "Good for a hundred sequins, O'Neilan," and placing it with my gold I began my bank.

The young officer was delighted, and said to me,

"Your bank might be defunct before the end of the sixth game."

I did not answer, and the play went on.

At the beginning of the fifth game, my bank was in the pangs of death; the young officer was in high glee. I rather astonished him by telling him that I was glad to lose, for I thought him a much more agreeable companion when he was winning.

There are some civilities which very likely prove unlucky for those to whom they are addressed, and it turned out so in this case, for my compliment turned his brain. During the fifth game, a run of adverse cards made him lose all he had won, and as he tried to do violence to Dame Fortune in the sixth round, he lost every sequin he had.

"Sir," he said to me, "you have been very lucky, but I hope you will give me my revenge to-morrow."

"It would be with the greatest pleasure, sir, but I never play except when I am under arrest."

I counted my money, and found that I had wan two hundred and fifty sequins, besides a debt of fifty sequins due by an officer who played on trust which Captain O'Neilan took on his own account. I completed his share, and at day-break he allowed me to go away.

As soon as I got to my hotel, I went to bed, and when I awoke, I had a visit from Captain Laurent, the officer who had played on trust. Thinking that his object was to pay me what he had lost, I told him that O'Neilan had taken his debt on himself, but he answered than he had only called for the purpose of begging of me a loan of six sequins on his note of hand, by which he would pledge his honour to repay me within one week. I gave him the money, and he begged that the matter, might remain between us.

"I promise it," I said to him, "but do not break your word."

The next day I was ill, and the reader is aware of the nature of my illness. I immediately placed myself under a proper course of diet, however unpleasant it was at my age; but I kept to my system, and it cured me rapidly.

Three or four days afterwards Captain O'Neilan called on me, and when I told him the nature of my sickness he laughed, much to my surprise.

"Then you were all right before that night?" he enquired.

"Yes, my health was excellent."

"I am sorry that you should have lost your health in such an ugly place. I would have warned you if I had thought you had any intentions in that quarter."

"Did you know of the woman having . . . ?"

"Zounds! Did I not? It is only a week since I paid a visit to the very same place myself, and I believe the creature was all right before my visit."

"Then I have to thank you for the present she has bestowed upon me."

"Most likely; but it is only a trifle, and you can easily get cured if you care to take the trouble."

"What! Do you not try to cure yourself?"

"Faith, no. It would be too much trouble to follow a regular diet, and what is the use of curing such a trifling inconvenience when I am certain of getting it again in a fortnight. Ten times in my life I have had that patience, but I got tired of it, and for the last two years I have resigned myself, and now I put up with it."

"I pity you, for a man like you would have great success in love."

"I do not care a fig for love; it requires cares which would bother me much more than the slight inconvenience to which we were alluding, and to which I am used now."

"I am not of your opinion, for the amorous pleasure is insipid when love does not throw a little spice in it. Do you think, for instance, that the ugly wretch I met at the guard-room is worth what I now suffer on her account?"

"Of course not, and that is why I am sorry for you. If I had known, I could have introduced you to something better."

"The very best in that line is not worth my health, and health ought to be sacrificed only for love."

"Oh! you want women worthy of love? There are a few here; stop with us for some time, and when you are cured there is nothing to prevent you from making conquests."

O'Neilan was only twenty-three years old; his father, who was dead, had been a general, and the beautiful Countess Borsati was his sister. He presented me to the Countess Zanardi Nerli, still more lovely than his sister, but I was prudent enough not to burn my incense before either of them, for it seemed to me that everybody could guess the state of my health.

I have never met a young man more addicted to debauchery than O'Neilan. I have often spent the night rambling about with him, and I was amazed at his cynical boldness and impudence. Yet he was noble, generous, brave, and honourable. If in those days young officers were often guilty of so much immorality, of so many vile actions, it was not so much their fault as the fault of the privileges which they enjoyed through custom, indulgence, or party spirit. Here is an example:

One day O'Neilan, having drunk rather freely, rides through the city at full speed. A poor old woman who was crossing the street has no time to avoid him, she falls, and her head is cut open by the horse's feet. O'Neilan places himself under arrest, but the next day he is set at liberty. He had, only to plead that it was an accident.

The officer Laurent not having called upon me to redeem his promisory note of six sequins during the week, I told him in the street that I would no longer consider myself bound to keep the affair secret. Instead of excusing himself, he said,

"I do not care!"

The answer was insulting, and I intended to compel him to give me reparation, but the next day O'Neilan told me that Captain Laurent had gone mad and had been locked up in a mad-house. He subsequently recovered his reason, but his conduct was so infamous that he was cashiered.

O'Neilan, who was as brave as Bayard, was killed a few years afterwards at the battle of Prague. A man of his complexion was certain to fall the victim of Mars or of Venus. He might be alive now if he had been endowed only with the courage of the fox, but he had the courage of the lion. It is a virtue in a soldier, but almost a fault in an officer. Those who brave danger with a full knowledge of it are worthy of praise, but those who do not realize it escape only by a miracle, and without any merit attaching itself to them. Yet we must respect those great warriors, for their unconquerable courage is the offspring of a strong soul, of a virtue which places them above ordinary mortals.

Whenever I think of Prince Charles de Ligne I cannot restrain my tears. He was as brave as Achilles, but Achilles was invulnerable. He would be alive now if he had remembered during the fight that he was mortal. Who are they that, having known him, have not shed tears in his memory? He was handsome, kind, polished, learned, a lover of the arts, cheerful, witty in his conversation, a pleasant companion, and a man of perfect equability. Fatal, terrible revolution! A cannon ball took him from his friends, from his family, from the happiness which surrounded him.

The Prince de Waldeck has also paid the penalty of his intrepidity with the loss of one arm. It is said that he consoles himself for that loss with the consciousness that with the remaining one he can yet command an army.

O you who despise life, tell me whether that contempt of life renders you worthy of it?

The opera opened immediately after Easter, and I was present at every performance. I was then entirely cured, and had resumed my usual life. I was pleased to see that Baletti shewed off Marina to the best advantage. I never visited her, but Baletti was in the habit of breakfasting with me almost every morning.

He had often mentioned an old actress who had left the stage for more than twenty years, and pretended to have been my father's friend. One day I took a fancy to call upon her, and he accompanied me to her house.

I saw an old, broken-down crone whose toilet astonished me as much as her person. In spite of her wrinkles, her face was plastered with red and white, and her eyebrows were indebted to India ink for their black appearance. She exposed one-half of her flabby, disgusting bosom, and there could be no doubt as to her false set of teeth. She wore a wig which fitted very badly, and allowed the intrusion of a few gray hairs which had survived the havoc of time. Her shaking hands made mine quiver when she pressed them. She diffused a perfume of amber at a distance of twenty yards, and her affected, mincing manner amused and sickened me at the same time. Her dress might possibly have been the fashion twenty years before. I was looking with dread at the fearful havoc of old age upon a face which, before merciless time had blighted it, had evidently been handsome, but what amazed me was the childish effrontery with which this time-withered specimen of womankind was still waging war with the help of her blasted charms.

Baletti, who feared lest my too visible astonishment should vex her, told her that I was amazed at the fact that the beautiful strawberry which bloomed upon her chest had not been withered by the hand of Time. It was a birth-mark which was really very much like a strawberry. "It is that mark," said the old woman, simpering, "which gave me the name of 'La Fragoletta.'"

Those words made me shudder.

I had before my eyes the fatal phantom which was the cause of my existence. I saw the woman who had thirty years before, seduced my father: if it had not been for her, he would never have thought of leaving his father's house, and would never have engendered me in the womb of a Venetian woman. I have never been of the opinion of the old author who says, 'Nemo vitam vellet si daretur scientibus'.

Seeing how thoughtful I was, she politely enquired my name from Baletti, for he had presented me only as a friend, and without having given her notice of my visit. When he told her that my name was Casanova, she was extremely surprised.

"Yes, madam," I said, "I am the son of Gaetan Casanova, of Parma."

"Heavens and earth! what is this? Ah! my friend, I adored your father! He was jealous without cause, and abandoned me. Had he not done so, you would have been my son! Allow me to embrace you with the feelings of a loving mother."

I expected as much, and, for fear she should fall, I went to her, received her kiss, and abandoned myself to her tender recollections. Still an actress, she pressed her handkerchief to her eyes, pretending to weep, and assuring me that I was not to doubt the truth of what she said.

"Although," she added, "I do not look an old woman yet."

"The only fault of your dear father," she continued, "was a want of gratitude."

I have no doubt that she passed the same sentence upon the son, for, in spite of her kind invitation, I never paid her another visit.

My purse was well filled, and as I did not care for Mantua, I resolved on going to Naples, to see again my dear Therese, Donna Lucrezia, Palo father and son, Don Antonio Casanova, and all my former acquaintances. However, my good genius did not approve of that decision, for I was not allowed to carry it into execution. I should have left Mantua three days later, had I not gone to the opera that night.

I lived like an anchorite during my two months' stay in Mantua, owing to the folly. I committed on the night of my arrival. I played only that time, and then I had been lucky. My slight erotic inconvenience, by compelling me to follow the diet necessary to my cure, most likely saved me from greater misfortunes which, perhaps, I should not have been able to avoid.

CHAPTER XXI

My Journey to Cesena in Search of Treasure—I Take Up My Quarters in Franzia's House— His Daughter Javotte

The opera was nearly over when I was accosted by a young man who, abruptly, and without any introduction, told me that as a stranger—I had been very wrong in spending two months in Mantua without paying a visit to the natural history collection belonging to his father, Don Antonio Capitani, commissary and prebendal president.

"Sir," I answered, "I have been guilty only through ignorance, and if you would be so good as to call for me at my hotel to-morrow morning, before the evening I shall have atoned for my error, and you will no longer have the right to address me the same reproach."

The son of the prebendal commissary called for me, and I found in his father a most eccentric, whimsical sort of man. The curiosities of his collection consisted of his family tree, of books of magic, relics, coins which he believed to be antediluvian, a model of the ark taken from nature at the time when Noah arrived in that extraordinary harbour, Mount Ararat, in Armenia. He load several medals, one of Sesostris, another of Semiramis, and an old knife of a queer shape, covered with rust. Besides all those wonderful treasures, he possessed, but under lock and key, all the paraphernalia of freemasonry.

"Pray, tell me," I said to him, "what relation there is between this collection and natural history? I see nothing here representing the three kingdoms."

"What! You do not see the antediluvian kingdom, that of Sesostris and that of Semiramis? Are not those the three kingdoms?"

When I heard that answer I embraced him with an exclamation of delight, which was sarcastic in its intent, but which he took for admiration, and he at once unfolded all the treasures of his whimsical knowledge respecting his possessions, ending with the rusty blade which he said was the very knife with which Saint Peter cut off the ear of Malek.

"What!" I exclaimed, "you are the possessor of this knife, and you are not as rich as Croesus?"

"How could I be so through the possession of the knife?"

"In two ways. In the first place, you could obtain possession of all the treasures hidden under ground in the States of the Church."

"Yes, that is a natural consequence, because St. Peter has the keys."

"In the second place, you might sell the knife to the Pope, if you happen to possess proof of its authenticity."

"You mean the parchment. Of course I have it; do you think I would have bought one without the other?"

"All right, then. In order to get possession of that knife, the Pope would, I have no doubt, make a cardinal of your son, but you must have the sheath too."

"I have not got it, but it is unnecessary. At all events I can have one made."

"That would not do, you must have the very one in which Saint Peter himself sheathed the knife when God said, 'Mitte gladium tuum in vaginam'. That very sheath does exist, and it is now in the hands of a person who might sell it to you at a reasonable price, or you might sell him your knife, for the sheath without the knife is of no use to him, just as the knife is useless to you without the sheath."

"How much would it cost me?"

"One thousand sequins."

"And how much would that person give me for the knife?"

"One thousand sequins, for one has as much value as the other."

The commissary, greatly astonished, looked at his son, and said, with the voice of a judge on the bench,

"Well, son, would you ever have thought that I would be offered one thousand sequins for this knife?"

He then opened a drawer and took out of it an old piece of paper, which he placed before me. It was written in Hebrew, and a facsimile of the knife was drawn on it. I pretended to be lost in admiration, and advised him very strongly to purchase the sheath.

"It is not necessary for me to buy it, or for your friend to purchase the knife. We can find out and dig up the treasures together."

"Not at all. The rubric says in the most forcible manner that the owner of the blade, 'in vaginam', shall be one. If the Pope were in possession of it he would be able, through a magical operation known to me, to cut off one of the ears of every Christian king who might be thinking of encroaching upon the rights of the Church."

"Wonderful, indeed! But it is very true, for it is said in the Gospel that Saint Peter did cut off the ear of somebody."

"Yes, of a king."

"Oh, no! not of a king."

"Of a king, I tell you. Enquire whether Malek or Melek does not mean king."

"Well! in case I should make up my mind to sell the knife, who would give me the thousand sequins?"

"I would; one half to-morrow, cash down; the balance of five hundred in a letter of exchange payable one month after date."

"Ah! that is like business. Be good enough, to accept a dish of macaroni with us to-morrow, and under a solemn pledge of secrecy we will discuss this important affair."

I accepted and took my leave, firmly resolved on keeping up the joke. I came back on the following day, and the very first thing he told me was that, to his certain knowledge, there was an immense treasure hidden somewhere in the Papal States, and that he would make up his mind to purchase the sheath. This satisfied me that there was no fear of his taking me at my word, so I produced a purse full of gold, saying I was quite ready to complete our bargain for the purchase of the knife.

"The Treasure," he said, "is worth millions; but let us have dinner. You are not going to be served in silver plates and dishes, but in real Raphael mosaic."

"My dear commissary, your magnificence astonishes me; mosaic is, indeed, by far superior to silver plate, although an ignorant fool would only consider it ugly earthen ware."

The compliment delighted him.

After dinner, he spoke as follows:

"A man in very good circumstances, residing in the Papal States, and owner of the country house in which he lives with all his family, is certain that there is a treasure in his cellar. He has written to my son, declaring himself ready to undertake all expenses necessary to possess himself of that treasure, if we could procure a magician powerful enough to unearth it."

The son then took a letter out of his pocket, read me some passages, and begged me to excuse him if, in consequence of his having pledged himself to keep the secret, he could not communicate all the contents of the letter; but I had, unperceived by him, read the word Cesena, the name of the village, and that was enough for me.

"Therefore all that is necessary is to give me the possibility of purchasing the sheath on credit, for I have no ready cash at present. You need not be afraid of endorsing my letters of exchange, and if you should know the magician you might go halves with him."

"The magician is ready; it is I, but unless you give me five hundred sequins cash down we cannot agree."

"I have no money."

"Then sell me the knife:"

"No."

"You are wrong, for now that I have seen it I can easily take it from you. But I am honest enough not to wish to play such a trick upon you."

"You could take my knife from me? I should like to be convinced of that, but I do not believe it."

"You do not? Very well, to-morrow the knife will be in my possession, but when it is once in my hands you need not hope to see it again. A spirit which is under my orders will bring it to me at midnight, and the same spirit will tell me where the treasure is buried:"

"Let the spirit tell you that, and I shall be convinced."

"Give me a pen, ink and paper."

I asked a question from my oracle, and the answer I had was that the treasure was to be found not far from the Rubicon.

"That is," I said, "a torrent which was once a river."

They consulted a dictionary, and found that the Rubicon flowed through Cesena. They were amazed, and, as I wished them to have full scope for wrong reasoning, I left them.

I had taken a fancy, not to purloin five hundred sequins from those poor fools, but to go and unearth the amount at their expense in the house of another fool, and to laugh at them all into the bargain. I longed to play the part of a magician. With that idea, when I left the house of the ridiculous antiquarian, I proceeded to the public library, where, with the assistance of a dictionary, I wrote the following specimen of facetious erudition:

"The treasure is buried in the earth at a depth of seventeen and a half fathoms, and has been there for six centuries. Its value amounts to two millions of sequins, enclosed in a casket, the same which was taken by Godfrey de Bouillon from Mathilda, Countess of Tuscany, in the year 1081, when he endeavoured to assist Henry IV, against that princess. He buried the box himself in the very spot where it now is, before he went to lay siege to Jerusalem. Gregory VII, who was a great magician, having been informed of the place where it had been hidden, had resolved on getting possession of it himself, but death prevented him from carrying out his intentions. After the death of the Countess Mathilda, in the year 1116, the genius presiding over all hidden treasures appointed seven spirits to guard the box. During a night with a full moon, a learned magician can raise the treasure to the surface of the earth by placing himself in the middle of the magical ring called maximus:"

I expected to see the father and son, and they came early in the morning.
After some rambling conversation, I gave them what I had composed at the
library, namely, the history of the treasure taken from the Countess
Mathilda.

I told them that I had made up my mind to recover the treasure, and I promised them the fourth part of it, provided they would purchase the sheath; I concluded by threatening again to possess myself of their knife.

"I cannot decide," said the commissary, "before I have seen the sheath."

"I pledge my word to shew it to you to-morrow," I answered.

We parted company, highly pleased with each other.

In order to manufacture a sheath, such as the wonderful knife required, it was necessary to combine the most whimsical idea with the oddest shape. I recollected very well the form of the blade, and, as I was revolving in my mind the best way to produce something very extravagant but well adapted to the purpose I had in view, I spied in the yard of the hotel an old piece of leather, the remnant of what had been a fine gentleman's boot; it was exactly what I wanted.

I took that old sole, boiled it, and made in it a slit in which I was certain that the knife would go easily. Then I pared it carefully on all sides to prevent the possibility of its former use being found out; I rubbed it with pumice stone, sand, and ochre, and finally I succeeded in imparting to my production such a queer, old-fashioned shape that I could not help laughing in looking at my work.

When I presented it to the commissary, and he had found it an exact fit for the knife, the good man remained astounded. We dined together, and after dinner it was decided that his son should accompany me, and introduce me to the master of the house in which the treasure was buried, that I was to receive a letter of exchange for one thousand Roman crowns, drawn by the son on Bologna, which would be made payable to my name only after I should have found the treasure, and that the knife with the sheath would be delivered into my hands only when I should require it for the great operation; until then the son was to retain possession of it.

Those conditions having been agreed upon, we made an agreement in writing, binding upon all parties, and our departure was fixed for the day after the morrow.

As we left Mantua, the father pronounced a fervent blessing over his son's head, and told me that he was count palatine, shewing me the diploma which he had received from the Pope. I embraced him, giving him his title of count, and pocketed his letter of exchange.

After bidding adieu to Marina, who was then the acknowledged mistress of Count Arcorati, and to Baletti whom I was sure of meeting again in Venice before the end of the year, I went to sup with my friend O'Neilan.

We started early in the morning, travelled through Ferrara and Bologna, and reached Cesena, where we put up at the posting-house. We got up early the next day and walked quietly to the house of George Franzia, a wealthy peasant, who was owner of the treasure. It was only a quarter of a mile from the city, and the good man was agreeably surprised by our arrival. He embraced Capitani, whom he knew already, and leaving me with his family he went out with my companion to talk business.

Observant as usual, I passed the family in review, and fixed my choice upon the eldest daughter. The youngest girl was ugly, and the son looked a regular fool. The mother seemed to be the real master of the household, and there were three or four servants going about the premises.

The eldest daughter was called Genevieve, or Javotte, a very common name among the girls of Cesena. I told her that I thought her eighteen; but she answered, in a tone half serious, half vexed, that I was very much mistaken, for she had only just completed her fourteenth year.

"I am very glad it is so, my pretty child."

These words brought back her smile.

The house was well situated, and there was not another dwelling around it for at least four hundred yards. I was glad to see that I should have comfortable quarters, but I was annoyed by a very unpleasant stink which tainted the air, and which could certainly not be agreeable to the spirits I had to evoke.

"Madame Franzia," said I, to the mistress of the house, "what is the cause of that bad smell?"

"Sir, it arises from the hemp which we are macerating."

I concluded that if the cause were removed, I should get rid of the effect.

"What is that hemp worth, madam?" I enquired.

"About forty crowns."

"Here they are; the hemp belongs to me now, and I must beg your husband to have it removed immediately."

Capitani called me, and I joined him. Franzia shewed me all the respect due to a great magician, although I had not much the appearance of one.

We agreed that he should receive one-fourth of the treasure, Capitani another fourth, and that the remainder should belong to me. We certainly did not shew much respect for the rights of Saint Peter.

I told Franzia that I should require a room with two beds for myself alone, and an ante-room with bathing apparatus. Capitani's room was to be in a different part of the house, and my room was to be provided with three tables, two of them small and one large. I added that he must at once procure me a sewing-girl between the ages of fourteen and eighteen, she was to be a virgin, and it was necessary that she should, as well as every person in the house, keep the secret faithfully, in order that no suspicion of our proceedings should reach the Inquisition, or all would be lost.

"I intend to take up my quarters here to-morrow," I added; "I require two meals every day, and the only wine I can drink is jevese. For my breakfast I drink a peculiar kind of chocolate which I make myself, and which I have brought with me. I promise to pay my own expenses in case we do not succeed. Please remove the hemp to a place sufficiently distant from the house, so that its bad smell may not annoy the spirits to be evoked by me, and let the air be purified by the discharge of gunpowder. Besides, you must send a trusty servant to-morrow to convey our luggage from the hotel here, and keep constantly in the house and at my disposal one hundred new wax candles and three torches."

After I had given those instructions to Franzia, I left him, and went towards Cesena with Capitani, but we had not gone a hundred yards when we heard the good man running after us.

"Sir," he said to me, "be kind enough to take back the forty crowns which you paid to my wife for the hemp."

"No, I will not do anything of the sort, for I do not want you to sustain any loss."

"Take them back, I beg. I can sell the hemp in the course of the day for forty crowns without difficulty."

"In that case I will, for I have confidence in what you say."

Such proceedings on my part impressed the excellent man very favourably, and he entertained the deepest veneration for me, which was increased, when, against Capitani's advice, I resolutely refused one hundred sequins which he wanted to force upon me for my travelling expenses. I threw him into raptures by telling him that on the eve of possessing an immense treasure, it was unnecessary to think of such trifles.

The next morning our luggage was sent for, and we found ourselves comfortably located in the house of the wealthy and simple Franzia.

He gave us a good dinner, but with too many dishes, and I told him to be more economical, and to give only some good fish for our supper, which he did. After supper he told me that, as far as the young maiden was concerned, he thought he could recommend his daughter Javotte, as he had consulted his wife, and had found I could rely upon the girl being a virgin.

"Very good," I said; "now tell me what grounds you have for supposing that there is a treasure in your house?"

"In the first place, the oral tradition transmitted from father to son for the last eight generations; in the second, the heavy sounds which are heard under ground during the night. Besides, the door of the cellar opens and shuts of itself every three or four minutes; which must certainly be the work of the devils seen every night wandering through the country in the shape of pyramidal flames."

"If it is as you say, it is evident that you have a treasure hidden somewhere in your house; it is as certain as the fact that two and two are four. Be very careful not to put a lock to the door of the cellar to prevent its opening and shutting of itself; otherwise you would have an earthquake, which would destroy everything here. Spirits will enjoy perfect freedom, and they break through every obstacle raised against them."

"God be praised for having sent here, forty years ago, a learned man who told my father exactly the same thing! That great magician required only three days more to unearth the treasure when my father heard that the Inquisition had given orders to arrest him, and he lost no time in insuring his escape. Can you tell me how it is that magicians are not more powerful than the Inquisitors?"

"Because the monks have a greater number of devils under their command than we have. But I feel certain that your father had already expended a great deal of money with that learned man."

"About two thousand crowns."

"Oh! more, more."

I told Franzia to follow me, and, in order to accomplish something in the magic line, I dipped a towel in some water, and uttering fearful words which belonged to no human language, I washed the eyes, the temples, and the chest of every person in the family, including Javotte, who might have objected to it if I had not begun with her father, mother, and brother. I made them swear upon my pocket-book that they were not labouring under any impure disease, and I concluded the ceremony by compelling Javotte to swear likewise that she had her maidenhood. As I saw that she was blushing to the very roots of her hair in taking the oath, I was cruel enough to explain to her what it meant; I then asked her to swear again, but she answered that there was no need of it now that she knew what it was. I ordered all the family to kiss me, and finding that Javotte had eaten garlic I forbade the use of it entirely, which order Franzia promised should be complied with.

Genevieve was not a beauty as far as her features were concerned; her complexion was too much sunburnt, and her mouth was too large, but her teeth were splendid, and her under lip projected slightly as if it had been formed to receive kisses. Her bosom was well made and as firm as a rock, but her hair was too light, and her hands too fleshy. The defects, however, had to be overlooked, and altogether she was not an unpleasant morsel. I did not purpose to make her fall in love with me; with a peasant girl that task might have been a long one; all I wanted was to train her to perfect obedience, which, in default of love, has always appeared to me the essential point. True that in such a case one does not enjoy the ecstatic raptures of love, but one finds a compensation in the complete control obtained over the woman.

I gave notice to the father, to Capitani, and to Javotte, that each would, in turn and in the order of their age, take supper with me, and that Javotte would sleep every night in my ante-room, where was to be placed a bath in which I would bathe my guest one half hour before sitting down to supper, and the guest was not to have broken his fast throughout the day.

I prepared a list of all the articles of which I pretended to be in need, and giving it to Franzia I told him to go to Cesena himself the next day, and to purchase everything without bargaining to obtain a lower price. Among other things, I ordered a piece, from twenty to thirty yards long, of white linen, thread, scissors, needles, storax, myrrh, sulphur, olive oil, camphor, one ream of paper, pens and ink, twelve sheets of parchment, brushes, and a branch of olive tree to make a stick of eighteen inches in length.

After I had given all my orders very seriously and without any wish to laugh, I went to bed highly pleased with my personification of a magician, in which I was astonished to find myself so completely successful.

The next morning, as soon as I was dressed, I sent for Capitani, and commanded him to proceed every day to Cesena, to go to the best coffee-house, to learn carefully every piece of news and every rumour, and to report them to me.

Franzia, who had faithfully obeyed my orders, returned before noon from the city with all the articles I had asked for.

"I have not bargained for anything," he said to me, "and the merchants must, I have no doubt, have taken me for a fool, for I have certainly paid one-third more than the things are worth."

"So much the worse for them if they have deceived you, but you would have spoilt everything if you had beaten them down in their price. Now, send me your daughter and let me be alone with her."

As soon as Javotte was in my room, I made her cut the linen in seven pieces, four of five feet long, two of two feet, and one of two feet and a half; the last one was intended to form the hood of the robe I was to wear for the great operation. Then I said to Javotte:

"Sit down near my bed and begin sewing. You will dine here and remain at work until the evening. When your father comes, you must let us be alone, but as soon as he leaves me, come back and go to bed."

She dined in my room, where her mother waited on her without speaking, and gave her nothing to drink except St. Jevese wine. Towards evening her father came, and she left us.

I had the patience to wash the good man while he was in the bath, after which he had supper with me; he ate voraciously, telling me that it was the first time in his life that he had remained twenty-four hours without breaking his fast. Intoxicated with the St. Jevese wine he had drunk, he went to bed and slept soundly until morning, when his wife brought me my chocolate. Javotte was kept sewing as on the day before; she left the room in the evening when Capitani came in, and I treated him in the same manner as

Franzia; on the third day, it was Javotte's turn, and that had been the object I had kept in view all the time.

When the hour came, I said to her,

"Go, Javotte, get into the bath and call me when you are ready, for I must purify you as I have purified your father and Capitani."

She obeyed, and within a quarter of an hour she called me. I performed a great many ablutions on every part of her body, making her assume all sorts of positions, for she was perfectly docile, but, as I was afraid of betraying myself, I felt more suffering than enjoyment, and my indiscreet hands, running over every part of her person, and remaining longer and more willingly on a certain spot, the sensitiveness of which is extreme, the poor girl was excited by an ardent fire which was at last quenched by the natural result of that excitement. I made her get out of the bath soon after that, and as I was drying her I was very near forgetting magic to follow the impulse of nature, but, quicker than I, nature relieved itself, and I was thus enabled to reach the end of the scene without anticipating the denouement. I told Javotte to dress herself, and to come back to me as soon as she was ready.

She had been fasting all day, and her toilet did not take a long time. She ate with a ferocious appetite, and the St. Jevese wine, which she drank like water, imparted so much animation to her complexion that it was no longer possible to see how sunburnt she was. Being alone with her after supper, I said to her,

"My dear Javotte, have you been displeased at all I have compelled you to submit to this evening?"

"Not at all; I liked it very much."

"Then I hope that you will have no objection to get in the bath with me to-morrow, and to wash me as I have washed you."

"Most willingly, but shall I know how to do it well?"

"I will teach you, and for the future I wish you to sleep every night in my room, because I must have a complete certainty that on the night of the great operation I shall find you such as you ought to be."

From that time Javotte was at her ease with me, all her restraint disappeared, she would look at me and smile with entire confidence. Nature had operated, and the mind of a young girl soon enlarges its sphere when pleasure is her teacher. She went to bed, and as she knew that she had no longer anything to conceal from me, her modesty was not alarmed when she undressed herself in my presence. It was very warm, any kind of covering is unpleasant in the hot weather, so she stripped to the skin and soon fell asleep. I did the same, but I could not help feeling some regret at having engaged myself not to take advantage of the position before the night of the great incantation. I knew that the operation to unearth the treasure would be a complete failure, but I knew likewise that it would not fail because Javotte's virginity was gone.

At day-break the girl rose and began sewing. As soon as she had finished the robe, I told her to make a crown of parchment with seven long points, on which I painted some fearful figures and hieroglyphs.

In the evening, one hour before supper, I got into the bath, and Javotte joined me as soon as I called her. She performed upon me with great zeal the same ceremonies that I had done for her the day before, and she was as gentle and docile as possible. I spent a delicious hour in that bath, enjoying everything, but respecting the essential point.

My kisses making her happy, and seeing that I had no objection to her caresses, she loaded me with them. I was so pleased at all the amorous enjoyment her senses were evidently experiencing, that I made her easy by telling her that the success of the great magic operation depended upon the amount of pleasure she enjoyed. She then made extraordinary efforts to persuade me that she was happy, and without overstepping the limits where I had made up my mind to stop, we got out of the bath highly pleased with each other.

As we were on the point of going to bed, she said to me,

"Would it injure the success of your operation if we were to sleep together?"

"No, my dear girl; provided you are a virgin on the day of the great incantation, it is all I require."

She threw herself in my arms, and we spent a delightful night, during which I had full opportunity of admiring the strength of her constitution as well as my own restraint, for I had sufficient control over myself not to break through the last obstacle.

I passed a great part of the following night with Franzia and Capitani in order to see with my own eyes the wonderful things which the worthy peasant had mentioned to me. Standing in the yard, I heard distinctly heavy blows struck under the ground at intervals of three or four minutes. It was like the noise which would be made by a heavy pestle falling in a large copper mortar. I took my pistols and placed myself near the self-moving door of the cellar, holding a dark lantern in my hand. I saw the door open slowly, and in about thirty seconds closing with violence. I opened and closed it myself several times, and, unable to discover any hidden physical cause for the phenomenon, I felt satisfied that there was some unknown roguery at work, but I did not care much to find it out.

We went upstairs again, and, placing myself on the balcony, I saw in the yard several shadows moving about. They were evidently caused by the heavy and damp atmosphere, and as to the pyramidal flames which I could see hovering over the fields, it was a phenomenon well known to me. But I allowed my two companions to remain persuaded that they were the spirits keeping watch over the treasure.

That phenomenon is very common throughout southern Italy where the country is often at night illuminated by those meteors which the people believe to be devils, and ignorance has called night spirits, or will-o'-the-wisps.

Dear reader, the next chapter will tell you how my magic undertaking ended, and perhaps you will enjoy a good laugh at my expense, but you need not be afraid of hurting my feelings.

CHAPTER XXII

The Incantation—A Terrible Storm—My Fright—Javotte's Virginity Is Saved—I Give Up the Undertaking, and Sell the Sheath to Capitani—I Meet Juliette and Count Alfani, Alias Count Celi—I Make Up My Mind to Go to Naples—Why I Take a Different Road

My great operation had to be performed on the following day; otherwise, according to all established rules, I would have had to wait until the next full moon. I had to make the gnomes raise the treasure to the surface of the earth at the very spot on which my incantations would be performed. Of course, I knew well enough that I should not succeed, but I knew likewise that I could easily reconcile Franzia and Capitani to a failure, by inventing some excellent reasons for our want of success. In the mean time I had to play my part of a magician, in which I took a real delight. I kept Javotte at work all day, sewing together, in the shape of a ring, some thirty sheets of paper on which I painted the most wonderful designs. That ring, which I called maximus, had a diameter of three geometric paces. I had manufactured a sort of sceptre or magic wand with the branch of olive brought by Franzia from Cesena. Thus prepared, I told Javotte that, at twelve o'clock at night, when I came out of the magic ring, she was to be ready for everything. The order did not seem repugnant to her; she longed to give me that proof of her obedience, and, on my side, considering myself as her debtor, I was in a hurry to pay my debt and to give her every satisfaction.

The hour having struck, I ordered Franzia and Capitani to stand on the balcony, so as to be ready to come to me if I called for them, and also to prevent anyone in the house seeing my proceedings. I then threw off all profane garments. I clothe myself in the long white robe, the work of a virgin's innocent hands. I allow my long hair to fall loosely. I place the extraordinary crown on my head, the circle maximus on my shoulders, and, seizing the sceptre with one hand, the wonderful knife with the other, I go down into the yard. There I spread my circle on the ground, uttering the most barbarous words, and after going round it three times I jump into the middle.

Squatting down there, I remain a few minutes motionless, then I rise, and I fix my eyes upon a heavy, dark cloud coming from the west, whilst from the same quarter the thunder is rumbling loudly. What a sublime genius I should have appeared in the eyes of my two fools, if, having a short time before taken notice of the sky in that part of the horizon, I had announced to them that my operation would be attended by that phenomenon.

The cloud spreads with fearful rapidity, and soon the sky seems covered with a funeral pall, on which the most vivid flashes of lightning keep blazing every moment.

Such a storm was a very natural occurrence, and I had no reason to be astonished at it, but somehow, fear was beginning to creep into me, and I wished myself in my room. My fright soon increased at the sight of the lightning, and on hearing the claps of thunder which succeeded each other with fearful rapidity and seemed to roar over my very head. I then realized what extraordinary effect fear can have on the mind, for I fancied that, if I was not annihilated by the fires of heaven which were flashing all around me, it was only because they could not enter my magic ring. Thus was I admiring my own deceitful work! That foolish reason prevented me from leaving the circle in spite of the fear which caused me to shudder. If it had not been for that belief, the result of a cowardly fright, I would not have remained one minute where I was, and my hurried flight would no doubt have opened the eyes of my two dupes, who could not have failed to see that, far from being a magician, I was only a poltroon. The violence of the wind, the claps of thunder, the piercing cold, and above all, fear, made me tremble all over like an aspen leaf. My system, which I thought proof against every accident, had vanished: I acknowledged an avenging God who had waited for this opportunity of punishing me at one blow for all my sins, and of annihilating me, in order to put an end to my want of faith. The complete immobility which paralyzed all my limbs seemed to me a proof of the uselessness of my repentance, and that conviction only increased my consternation.

But the roaring of the thunder dies away, the rain begins to fall heavily, danger vanishes, and I feel my courage reviving. Such is man! or at all events, such was I at that moment. It was raining so fast that, if it had continued pouring with the same violence for a quarter of an hour, the country would have been inundated. As soon as the rain had ceased, the wind abated, the clouds were dispersed, and the moon shone in all its splendour, like silver in the pure, blue sky. I take up my magic ring, and telling the two friends to retire to their beds without speaking to me, I hurry to my room. I still felt rather shaken, and, casting my eyes on Javotte, I thought her so pretty that I felt positively frightened. I allowed her to dry me, and after that necessary operation I told her piteously to go to bed. The next morning she told me that, when she saw me come in, shaking all over in spite of the heat, she had herself shuddered with fear.

After eight hours of sound sleep I felt all right, but I had had enough of the comedy, and to my great surprise the sight of Genevieve did not move me in any way. The obedient Javotte had certainly not changed, but I was not the same. I was for the first time in my life reduced to a state of apathy, and in consequence of the superstitious ideas which had crowded in my mind the previous night I imagined that the innocence of that young girl was under the special protection of Heaven, and that if I had dared to rob her of her virginity the most rapid and terrible death would have been my punishment.

At all events, thanks to my youth and my exalted ideas, I fancied that through my self-denying resolutions the father would not be so great a dupe, and the daughter not so unhappy, unless the result should prove as unfortunate for her as it had been for poor Lucy, of Pasean.

The moment that Javotte became in my eyes an object of holy horror, my departure was decided. The resolution was all the more irrevocable because I fancied some old peasant might have witnessed all my tricks in the middle of the magic ring, in which case the most Holy, or, if you like, the most infernal, Inquisition, receiving information from him, might very well have caught me and enhanced my fame by some splendid 'auto-da-fe' in which I had not the slightest wish to be the principal actor. It struck me as so entirely within the limits of probability that I sent at once for Franzia and Capitani, and in the presence of the unpolluted virgin I told them that I had obtained from the seven spirits watching over the treasure all the necessary particulars, but that I had been compelled to enter into an agreement with them to delay the extraction of the treasure placed under their guardianship. I told Franzia that I would hand to him in writing all the information which I had compelled the spirits to give me. I produced, in reality, a few minutes afterwards, a document similar to the one I had concocted at the public library in Mantua, adding that the treasure consisted of diamonds, rubies, emeralds, and one hundred thousand pounds of gold dust. I made him take an oath on my pocket-book to wait for me, and not to have faith in any magician unless he gave him an account of the treasure in every way similar to the one which, as a great favor, I was leaving in his hands. I ordered him to burn the crown and the ring, but to keep the other things carefully until my return.

"As for you, Capitani," I said to my companion, "proceed at once to Cesena, and remain at the inn until our luggage has been brought by the man whom Franzia is going to send with it."

Seeing that poor Javotte looked miserable, I went up to her, and, speaking to her very tenderly, I promised to see her again before long. I told her at the same time that, the great operation having been performed successfully, her virginity was no longer necessary, and that she was at liberty to marry as soon as she pleased, or whenever a good opportunity offered itself.

I at once returned to the city, where I found Capitani making his preparations to go to the fair of Lugo, and then to Mantua. He told me, crying like a child, that his father would be in despair when he saw him come back without the knife of Saint Peter.

"You may have it," I said, "with the sheath, if you will let me have the one thousand Roman crowns, the amount of the letter of exchange."

He thought it an excellent bargain, and accepted it joyfully. I gave him back the letter of exchange, and made him sign a paper by which he undertook to return the sheath whenever I brought the same amount, but he is still waiting for it.

I did not know what to do with the wonderful sheath, and I was not in want of money, but I should have considered myself dishonoured if I had given it to him for nothing; besides, I thought it a good joke to levy a contribution upon the ignorant credulity of a count palatine created by the grace of the Pope. In after days, however, I would willingly have refunded his money, but, as fate would have it, we did not see each other for a long time, and when I met him again I was not in a position to return the amount. It is, therefore, only to chance that I was indebted for the sum, and certainly Capitani never dreamed of complaining, for being the possessor of 'gladium cum vagina' he truly believed himself the master of every treasure concealed in the Papal States.

Capitani took leave of me on the following day, and I intended to proceed at once to Naples, but I was again prevented; this is how it happened.

As I returned to the inn after a short walk, mine host handed me the bill of the play announcing four performances of the Didone of Metastasio at the Spada. Seeing no acquaintance of mine among the actors or actresses, I made up my mind to go to the play in the evening, and to start early the next day with post-horses. A remnant of my fear of the Inquisition urged me on, and I could not help fancying that spies were at my heels.

Before entering the house I went into the actresses dressing-room, and the leading lady struck me as rather good-looking. Her name was Narici, and she was from Bologna. I bowed to her, and after the common-place conversation usual in such cases, I asked her whether she was free.

"I am only engaged with the manager," she answered.

"Have you any lover?"

"No."

"I offer myself for the post, if you have no objection."

She smiled jeeringly, and said,

"Will you take four tickets for the four performances?"

I took two sequins out of my purse, taking care to let her see that it was well filled, and when she gave me the four tickets, presented them to the maid who was dressing her and was prettier than the mistress, and so left the room without uttering a single word. She called me back; I pretended not to hear her, and took a ticket for the pit. After the first ballet, finding the whole performance very poor,

I was thinking of going away, when, happening to look towards the chief box, I saw to my astonishment that it was tenanted by the Venetian Manzoni and the celebrated Juliette. The reader will doubtless remember the ball she gave at my house in Venice, and the smack with which she saluted my cheek on that occasion.

They had not yet noticed me, and I enquired from the person seated next to me who was that beautiful lady wearing so many diamonds. He told me that she was Madame Querini, from Venice, whom Count Spada, the owner of the theatre, who was sitting near her, had brought with him from Faenza. I was glad to hear that M. Querini had married her at last, but I did not think of renewing the acquaintance, for reasons which my reader cannot have forgotten if he recollects our quarrel when I had to dress her as an abbe. I was on the point of going away when she happened to see me and called me. I went up to her, and, not wishing to be known by anyone, I whispered to her that my name was Farusi. Manzoni informed me that I was speaking to her excellency, Madame Querini. "I know it," I said, "through a letter which I have received from Venice, and I beg to offer my most sincere congratulations to Madame." She heard me and introduced me to Count Spada, creating me a baron on the spot. He invited me most kindly to come to his box, asked me where I came from, where I was going to, etc., and begged the pleasure of my company at supper for the same evening.

Ten years before, he had been Juliette's friend in Vienna, when Maria Theresa, having been informed of the pernicious influence of her beauty, gave her notice to quit the city. She had renewed her acquaintance with him in Venice, and had contrived to make him take her to Bologna on a pleasure trip. M. Manzoni, her old follower, who gave me all this information, accompanied her in order to bear witness of her good conduct before M. Querini. I must say that Manzoni was not a well-chosen chaperon.

In Venice she wanted everybody to believe that Querini had married her secretly, but at a distance of fifty leagues she did not think such a formality necessary, and she had already been presented by the general to all the nobility of Cesena as Madame Querini Papozzes. M. Querini would have been wrong in being jealous of the count, for he was an old acquaintance who would do no harm. Besides, it is admitted amongst certain women that the reigning lover who is jealous of an old acquaintance is nothing but a fool, and ought to be treated as such. Juliette, most likely afraid of my being indiscreet, had lost no time in making the first advances, but, seeing that I had likewise some reason to fear her want of discretion, she felt reassured. From the first moment I treated her politely, and with every consideration due to her position.

I found numerous company at the general's, and some pretty women. Not seeing Juliette, I enquired for her from M. Manzoni, who told me that she was at the faro table, losing her money. I saw her seated next to the banker, who turned pale at the sight of my face. He was no other than the so-called Count Celi. He offered me a card, which I refused politely, but I accepted Juliette's offer to be her partner. She had about fifty sequins, I handed her the same sum, and took a seat near her. After the first round, she asked me if I knew the banker; Celi had heard the question; I answered negatively. A lady on my left told me that the banker was Count

Alfani. Half an hour later, Madame Querini went seven and lost, she increased her stake of ten sequins; it was the last deal of the game, and therefore the decisive one. I rose from my chair, and fixed my eyes on the banker's hands. But in spite of that, he cheated before me, and Madame lost.

Just at that moment the general offered her his arm to go to supper; she left the remainder of her gold on the table, and after supper, having played again, she lost every sequin.

I enlivened the supper by my stories and witty jests. I captivated everybody's friendship, and particularly the general's, who, having heard me say that I was going to Naples only to gratify an amorous fancy, entreated me to spend a month with him and to sacrifice my whim. But it was all in vain. My heart was unoccupied; I longed to see Lucrezia and Therese, whose charms after five years I could scarcely recollect. I only consented to remain in Cesena the four days during which the general intended to stay.

The next morning as I was dressing I had a call from the cowardly Alfani-Celi; I received him with a jeering smile, saying that I had expected him.

The hair-dresser being in the room Celi did not answer, but as soon as we were alone he said,

"How could you possibly expect my visit?"

"I will tell you my reason as soon as you have handed me one hundred sequins, and you are going to do so at once.'

"Here are fifty which I brought for you; you cannot demand more from me."

"Thank you, I take them on account, but as I am good-natured I advise you not to shew yourself this evening in Count Spada's drawing-rooms, for you would not be admitted, and it would be owing to me."

"I hope that you will think twice before you are guilty of such an ungenerous act."

"I have made up my mind; but now leave me."

There was a knock at my door, and the self-styled Count Alfani went away without giving me the trouble of repeating my order. My new visitor proved to be the first castrato of the theatre, who brought an invitation to dinner from Narici. The invitation was curious, and I accepted it with a smile. The castrato was named Nicolas Peritti; he pretended to be the grandson of a natural child of Sixtus V.; it might have been so I shall have to mention him again in fifteen years.

When I made my appearance at Narici's house I saw Count Alfani, who certainly did not expect me, and must have taken me for his evil genius. He bowed to me with great politeness, and begged that I would listen to a few words in private.

"Here are fifty sequins more," he said; "but as an honest man you can take them only to give them to Madame Querini. But how can you hand the amount to her without letting her know that you have forced me to refund it? You understand what consequences such a confession might have for me."

"I shall give her the money only when you have left this place; in the mean time I promise to be discreet, but be careful not to assist fortune in my presence, or I must act in a manner that will not be agreeable to you."

"Double the capital of my bank, and we can be partners."

"Your proposal is an insult."

He gave me fifty sequins, and I promised to keep his secret.

There was a numerous attendance in Narici's rooms, especially of young men, who after dinner lost all their money. I did not play, and it was a disappointment for my pretty hostess, who had invited me only because she had judged me as simple as the others. I remained an indifferent witness of the play, and it gave me an opportunity of realizing how wise Mahomet had been in forbidding all games of chance.

In the evening after the opera Count Celi had the faro bank, and I lose two hundred sequins, but I could only accuse ill luck. Madame Querini won. The next day before supper I broke the bank, and after supper, feeling tired and well pleased with what I had won, I returned to the inn.

The following morning, which was the third day, and therefore the last but one of my stay in Cesena, I called at the general's. I heard that his adjutant had thrown the cards in Alfani's face, and that a meeting had been arranged between them for twelve o'clock. I went to the adjutant's room and offered to be his second, assuring him that there would be no blood spilt. He declined my offer with many thanks, and at dinner-time he told me that I had guessed rightly, for Count Alfani had left for Rome.

"In that case," I said to the guests, "I will take the bank tonight."

After dinner, being alone with Madame Querini, I told her all about Alfani, alias Celi, and handed her the fifty sequins of which I was the depositary.

"I suppose," she said, "that by means of this fable you hope to make me accept fifty sequins, but I thank you, I am not in want of money."

"I give you my word that I have compelled the thief to refund this money, together with the fifty sequins of which he had likewise cheated me."

"That may be, but I do not wish to believe you. I beg to inform you that I am not simple enough to allow myself to be duped, and, what is worse, cheated in such a manner."

Philosophy forbids a man to feel repentance for a good deed, but he must certainly have a right to regret such a deed when it is malevolently misconstrued, and turned against him as a reproach.

In the evening, after the performance, which was to be the last, I took the bank according to my promise: I lost a few sequins, but was caressed by everybody, and that is much more pleasant than winning, when we are not labouring under the hard necessity of making money.

Count Spada, who had got quite fond of me, wanted me to accompany him to Brisighetta, but I resisted his entreaties because I had firmly resolved on going to Naples.

The next morning I was awoke by a terrible noise in the passage, almost at the door of my room.

Getting out of my bed, I open my door to ascertain the cause of the uproar. I see a troop of 'sbirri' at the door of a chamber, and in that chamber, sitting up in bed, a fine-looking man who was making himself hoarse by screaming in Latin against that rabble, the plague of Italy, and against the inn-keeper who had been rascally enough to open the door.

I enquire of the inn-keeper what it all means.

"This gentleman," answers the scoundrel, "who, it appears, can only speak Latin, is in bed with a girl, and the 'sbirri' of the bishop have been sent to know whether she is truly his wife; all perfectly regular. If she is his wife, he has only to convince them by shewing a certificate of marriage, but if she is not, of course he must go to prison with her. Yet it need not happen, for I undertake to arrange everything in a friendly manner for a few sequins. I have only to exchange a few words with the chief of the 'sbirri', and they will all go away. If you can speak Latin, you had better go in, and make him listen to reason."

"Who has broken open the door of his room?"

"Nobody; I have opened it myself with the key, as is my duty."

"Yes, the duty of a highway robber, but not of an honest inn-keeper."

Such infamous dealing aroused my indignation, and I made up my mind to interfere. I enter the room, although I had still my nightcap on, and inform the gentleman of the cause of the disturbance. He answers with a laugh that, in the first place, it was impossible to say whether the person who was in bed with him was a woman, for that person had only been seen in the costume of a military officer, and that, in the second place, he did not think that any human being had a right to compel him to say whether his bed-fellow was his wife or his mistress, even supposing that his companion was truly a woman.

"At all events," he added, "I am determined not to give one crown to arrange the affair, and to remain in bed until my door is shut. The moment I am dressed, I will treat you to an amusing denouement of the comedy. I will drive away all those scoundrels at the point of my sword."

I then see in a corner a broad sword, and a Hungarian costume looking like a military uniform. I ask whether he is an officer.

"I have written my name and profession," he answers, "in the hotel book."

Astonished at the absurdity of the inn-keeper, I ask him whether it is so; he confesses it, but adds that the clergy have the right to prevent scandal.

"The insult you have offered to that officer, Mr. Landlord, will cost you very dear."

His only answer is to laugh in my face. Highly enraged at seeing such a scoundrel laugh at me, I take up the officer's quarrel warmly, and asked him to entrust his passport to me for a few minutes.

"I have two," he says; "therefore I can let you have one." And taking the document out of his pocket-book, he hands it to me. The passport was signed by Cardinal Albani. The officer was a captain in a Hungarian regiment belonging to the empress and queen. He was from Rome, on his way to Parma with dispatches from Cardinal Albani Alexander to M. Dutillot, prime minister of the Infante of Parma.

At the same moment, a man burst into the room, speaking very loudly, and asked me to tell the officer that the affair must be settled at once, because he wanted to leave Cesena immediately.

"Who are you?" I asked the man.

He answered that he was the 'vetturino' whom the captain had engaged. I saw that it was a regular put-up thing, and begged the captain to let me attend to the business, assuring him that I would settle it to his honour and advantage.

"Do exactly as you please," he said.

Then turning towards the 'vetturino', I ordered him to bring up the captain's luggage, saying that he would be paid at once. When he had done so, I handed him eight sequins out of my own purse, and made him give me a receipt in the name of the captain, who could only speak German, Hungarian, and Latin. The vetturino went away, and the 'sbirri' followed him in the greatest consternation, except two who remained.

"Captain," I said to the Hungarian, "keep your bed until I return. I am going now to the bishop to give him an account of these proceedings, and make him understand that he owes you some reparation. Besides, General Spada is here, and...."

"I know him," interrupted the captain, "and if I had been aware of his being in Cesena, I would have shot the landlord when he opened my door to those scoundrels."

I hurried over my toilet, and without waiting for my hair to be dressed I proceeded to the bishop's palace, and making a great deal of noise I almost compelled the servants to take me to his room. A lackey who was at the door informed me that his lordship was still in bed.

"Never mind, I cannot wait."

I pushed him aside and entered the room. I related the whole affair to the bishop, exaggerating the uproar, making much of the injustice of such proceedings, and railing at a vexatious police daring to molest travellers and to insult the sacred rights of individuals and nations.

The bishop without answering me referred me to his chancellor, to whom I repeated all I had said to the bishop, but with words calculated to irritate rather than to soften, and certainly not likely to obtain the release of the captain. I even went so far as to threaten, and I said that if I were in the place of the officer I would demand a public reparation. The priest laughed at my threats; it was just what I wanted, and after asking me whether I had taken leave of my senses, the chancellor told me to apply to the captain of the 'sbirri'.

"I shall go to somebody else," I said, "reverend sir, besides the captain of the 'sbirri'."

Delighted at having made matters worse, I left him and proceeded straight to the house of General Spada, but being told that he could not be seen before eight o'clock, I returned to the inn.

The state of excitement in which I was, the ardour with which I had made the affair mine, might have led anyone to suppose that my indignation had been roused only by disgust at seeing an odious persecution perpetrated upon a stranger by an unrestrained, immoral, and vexatious police; but why should I deceive the kind reader, to whom I have promised to tell the truth; I must therefore say that my indignation was real, but my ardour was excited by another feeling of a more personal nature. I fancied that the woman concealed under the bed-clothes was a beauty. I longed to see her face, which shame, most likely, had prevented her from shewing. She had heard me speak, and the good opinion that I had of myself did not leave the shadow of a doubt in my mind that she would prefer me to her captain.

The door of the room being still open, I went in and related to the captain all I had done, assuring him that in the course of the day he would be at liberty to continue his journey at the bishop's expense, for the general would not fail to obtain complete satisfaction for him. He thanked me warmly, gave back the eight ducats I had paid for him, and said that he would not leave the city till the next day.

"From what country," I asked him, "is your travelling companion?"

"From France, and he only speaks his native language."

"Then you speak French?"

"Not one word."

"That is amusing! Then you converse in pantomime?"

"Exactly."

"I pity you, for it is a difficult language."

"Yes, to express the various shades of thought, but in the material part of our intercourse we understand each other quite well."

"May I invite myself to breakfast with you?"

"Ask my friend whether he has any objection."

"Amiable companion of the captain," I said in French, "will you kindly accept me as a third guest at the breakfast-table?"

At these words I saw coming out of the bed-clothes a lovely head, with dishevelled hair, and a blooming, laughing face which, although it was crowned with a man's cap, left no doubt that the captain's friend belonged to that sex without which man would be the most miserable animal on earth.

Delighted with the graceful creature, I told her that I had been happy enough to feel interested in her even before I had seen her, and that now that I had the pleasure of seeing her, I could but renew with greater zeal all my efforts to serve her.

She answered me with the grace and the animation which are the exclusive privilege of her native country, and retorted my argument in the most witty manner; I was already under the charm. My request was granted; I went out to order breakfast, and to give them an opportunity of making themselves comfortable in bed, for they were determined not to get up until the door of their room was closed again.

The waiter came, and I went in with him. I found my lovely Frenchwoman wearing a blue frock-coat, with her hair badly arranged like a man's, but very charming even in that strange costume. I longed to see her up. She ate her breakfast without once interrupting the officer speaking to me, but to whom I was not listening, or listening with very little attention, for I was in a sort of ecstatic trance.

Immediately after breakfast, I called on the general, and related the affair to him, enlarging upon it in such a manner as to pique his martial pride. I told him that, unless he settled the matter himself, the Hungarian captain was determined to send an express to the cardinal immediately. But my eloquence was unnecessary, for the general liked to see priests attend to the business of Heaven, but he could not bear them to meddle in temporal affairs.

"I shall," he said, "immediately put a stop to this ridiculous comedy, and treat it in a very serious manner."

"Go at once to the inn," he said to his aide-de-camp, "invite that officer and his companion to dine with me to-day, and repair afterwards to the bishop's palace. Give him notice that the officer who has been so grossly insulted by his 'sbirri' shall not leave the city before he has received a complete apology, and whatever sum of money he may claim as damages. Tell him that the notice comes from me, and that all the expenses incurred by the officer shall be paid by him."

What pleasure it was for me to listen to these words! In my vanity, I fancied I had almost prompted them to the general. I accompanied the aide-de-camp, and introduced him to the captain who received him with the joy of a soldier meeting a comrade. The adjutant gave him the general's invitation for him and his companion, and asked him to write down what satisfaction he wanted, as well as the amount of damages he claimed. At the sight of the general's adjutant, the 'sbirri' had quickly vanished. I handed to the captain pen, paper and ink, and he wrote his claim in pretty good Latin for a native of Hungary. The excellent fellow absolutely refused to ask for more than thirty sequins, in spite of all I said to make him claim one hundred. He was likewise a great deal too easy as to the satisfaction he demanded, for all he asked was to see the landlord and the 'sbirri' beg his pardon on their knees in the presence of the general's adjutant. He threatened the bishop to send an express to Rome to Cardinal Alexander, unless his demands were complied with within two hours, and to remain in Cesena at the rate of ten sequins a day at the bishop's expense.

The officer left us, and a moment afterwards the landlord came in respectfully, to inform the captain that he was free, but the captain having begged me to tell the scoundrel that he owed him a sound thrashing, he lost no time in gaining the door.

I left my friends alone to get dressed, and to attend to my own toilet, as I dined with them at the general's. An hour afterwards I found them ready in their military costumes. The uniform of the Frenchwoman was of course a fancy one, but very elegant. The moment I saw her, I gave up all idea of Naples, and decided upon accompanying the two friends to Parma. The beauty of the lovely Frenchwoman had already captivated me. The captain was certainly on the threshold of sixty, and, as a matter of course, I thought such a union very badly assorted. I imagined that the affair which I was already concocting in my brain could be arranged amicably.

The adjutant came back with a priest sent by the bishop, who told the captain that he should have the satisfaction as well as the damages he had claimed, but that he must be content with fifteen sequins.

"Thirty or nothing," dryly answered the Hungarian.

They were at last given to him, and thus the matter ended. The victory was due to my exertions, and I had won the friendship of the captain and his lovely companion.

In order to guess, even at first sight, that the friend of the worthy captain was not a man, it was enough to look at the hips. She was too well made as a woman ever to pass for a man, and the women who disguise themselves in male attire, and boast of being like men, are very wrong, for by such a boast they confess themselves deficient in one of the greatest perfections appertaining to woman.

A little before dinner-time we repaired to General Spada's mansion, and the general presented the two officers to all the ladies. Not one of them was deceived in the young officer, but, being already acquainted with the adventure, they were all delighted to dine with the hero of the comedy, and treated the handsome officer exactly as if he had truly been a man, but I am bound to confess that the male guests offered the Frenchwoman homages more worthy of her sex.

Madame Querini alone did not seem pleased, because the lovely stranger monopolized the general attention, and it was a blow to her vanity to see herself neglected. She never spoke to her, except to shew off her French, which she could speak well. The poor captain scarcely opened his lips, for no one cared to speak Latin, and the general had not much to say in German.

An elderly priest, who was one of the guests, tried to justify the conduct of the bishop by assuring us that the inn-keeper and the 'sbirri' had acted only under the orders of the Holy Office.

"That is the reason," he said, "for which no bolts are allowed in the rooms of the hotels, so that strangers may not shut themselves up in their chambers. The Holy Inquisition does not allow a man to sleep with any woman but his wife."

Twenty years later I found all the doors in Spain with a bolt outside, so that travellers were, as if they had been in prison, exposed to the outrageous molestation of nocturnal visits from the police. That disease is so chronic in Spain that it threatens to overthrow the monarchy some day, and I should not be astonished if one fine morning the Grand Inquisitor was to have the king shaved, and to take his place.

CHAPTER XXIII

I Purchase a Handsome Carriage, and Proceed to Parma With the Old Captain and the Young Frenchwoman—I Pay a Visit to Javotte, and Present Her With a Beautiful Pair of Gold Bracelets—My Perplexities Respecting My Lovely Travelling Companion—A Monologue—Conversation with the Captain—Tete-a-Tete with Henriette

The conversation was animated, and the young female officer was entertaining everybody, even Madame Querini, although she hardly took the trouble of concealing her spleen.

"It seems strange," she remarked, "that you and the captain should live together without ever speaking to each other."

"Why, madam? We understand one another perfectly, for speech is of very little consequence in the kind of business we do together."

That answer, given with graceful liveliness, made everybody laugh, except Madame Querini-Juliette, who, foolishly assuming the air of a prude, thought that its meaning was too clearly expressed.

"I do not know any kind of business," she said, "that can be transacted without the assistance of the voice or the pen."

"Excuse me, madam, there are some: playing at cards, for instance, is a business of that sort."

"Are you always playing?"

"We do nothing else. We play the game of the Pharaoh (faro), and I hold the bank."

Everybody, understanding the shrewdness of this evasive answer, laughed again, and Juliette herself could not help joining in the general merriment.

"But tell me," said Count Spada, "does the bank receive much?"

"As for the deposits, they are of so little importance, that they are hardly worth mentioning."

No one ventured upon translating that sentence for the benefit of the worthy captain. The conversation continued in the same amusing style, and all the guests were delighted with the graceful wit of the charming officer.

Late in the evening I took leave of the general, and wished him a pleasant journey.

"Adieu," he said, "I wish you a pleasant journey to Naples, and hope you will enjoy yourself there."

"Well, general, I am not going to Naples immediately; I have changed my mind and intend to proceed to Parma, where I wish to see the Infante. I also wish to constitute myself the interpreter of these two officers who know nothing of Italian."

"Ah, young man! opportunity makes a thief, does it not? Well, if I were in your place, I would do the same."

I also bade farewell to Madame Querini, who asked me to write to her from

Bologna. I gave her a promise to do so, but without meaning to fulfil it.

I had felt interested in the young Frenchwoman when she was hiding under the bed-clothes: she had taken my fancy the moment she had shewn her features, and still more when I had seen her dressed. She completed her conquest at the dinner-table by the display of a wit which I greatly admired. It is rare in Italy, and seems to belong generally to the daughters of France. I did not think it would be very difficult to win her love, and I resolved on trying. Putting my self-esteem on one side, I fancied I would suit her much better than the old Hungarian, a very pleasant man for his age, but who, after all, carried his sixty years on his face, while my twenty-three were blooming on my countenance. It seemed to me that the captain himself would not raise any great objection, for he seemed one of those men who, treating love as a matter of pure fancy, accept all circumstances easily, and give way good-naturedly to all the freaks of fortune. By becoming the travelling companion of this ill-matched couple, I should probably succeed in my aims. I never dreamed of experiencing a refusal at their hands, my company would certainly be agreeable to them, as they could not exchange a single word by themselves.

With this idea I asked the captain, as we reached our inn, whether he intended to proceed to Parma by the public coach or otherwise.

"As I have no carriage of my own," he answered, "we shall have to take the coach."

"I have a very comfortable carriage, and I offer you the two back seats if you have no objection to my society."

"That is a piece of good fortune. Be kind enough to propose it to Henriette."

"Will you, madam, grant me the favour of accompanying you to Parma?"

"I should be delighted, for we could have some conversation, but take care, sir, your task will not be an easy one, you will often find yourself obliged to translate for both of us."

"I shall do so with great pleasure; I am only sorry that the journey is not longer. We can arrange everything at supper-time; allow me to leave you now as I have some business to settle."

My business was in reference to a carriage, for the one I had boasted of existed only in my imagination. I went to the most fashionable coffee-house, and, as good luck would have it, heard that there was a travelling carriage for sale, which no one would buy because it was too expensive. Two hundred sequins were asked for it, although it had but two seats and a bracket-stool for a third person. It was just what I wanted. I called at the place where it would be seen. I found a very fine English carriage which could not have cost less than two hundred guineas. Its noble proprietor was then at supper, so I sent him my name, requesting him not to dispose of his carriage until the next morning, and I went back to the hotel well pleased with my discovery. At supper I arranged with the captain that we would not leave Cesena till after dinner on the following day, and the conversation was almost entirely a dialogue between Henriette and myself; it was my first talk with a French woman. I thought this young creature more and more charming, yet I could not suppose her to be anything else but an adventurers, and I was astonished at discovering in her those noble and delicate feelings which denote a good education. However, as such an idea would not have suited the views I had about her, I rejected it whenever it presented itself to my mind. Whenever I tried to make her talk about the captain she would change the subject of conversation, or evade my insinuations with a tact and a shrewdness which astonished and delighted me at the same time, for everything she said bore the impress of grace and wit. Yet she did not elude this question:

"At least tell me, madam, whether the captain is your husband or your father."

"Neither one nor the other," she answered, with a smile.

That was enough for me, and in reality what more did I want to know? The worthy captain had fallen asleep. When he awoke I wished them both good night, and retired to my room with a heart full of love and a mind full of projects. I saw that everything had taken a good turn, and I felt certain of success, for I was young, I enjoyed excellent health, I had money and plenty of daring. I liked the affair all the better because it must come to a conclusion in a few days.

Early the next morning I called upon Count Dandini, the owner of the carriage, and as I passed a jeweller's shop I bought a pair of gold bracelets in Venetian filigree, each five yards long and of rare fineness. I intended them as a present for Javotte.

The moment Count Dandini saw me he recognized me. He had seen me in Padua at the house of his father, who was professor of civil law at the time I was a student there. I bought his carriage on condition that he would send it to me in good repair at one o'clock in the afternoon.

Having completed the purchase, I went to my friend, Franzia, and my present of the bracelets made Javotte perfectly happy. There was not one girl in Cesena who could boast of possessing a finer pair, and with that present my conscience felt at ease, for it paid the expense I had occasioned during my stay of ten or twelve days at her father's house four times over. But this was not the most important present I offered the family. I made the father take an oath to wait for me, and never to trust in any pretended magician for the necessary operation to obtain the treasure, even if I did not return or give any news of myself for ten years.

"Because," I said to him, "in consequence of the agreement in which I have entered with the spirits watching the treasure, at the first attempt made by any other person, the casket containing the treasure will sink to twice its present depth, that is to say as deep as thirty-five fathoms, and then I shall have myself ten times more difficulty in raising it to the surface. I cannot state precisely the time of my return, for it depends upon certain combinations which are not under my control, but recollect that the treasure cannot be obtained by anyone but I."

I accompanied my advice with threats of utter ruin to his family if he should ever break his oath. And in this manner I atoned for all I had done, for, far from deceiving the worthy man, I became his benefactor by guarding against the deceit of some cheat who would have cared for his money more than for his daughter. I never saw him again, and most likely he is dead, but knowing the deep impression I left on his mind I am certain that his descendants are even now waiting for me, for the name of Farusi must have remained immortal in that family.

Javotte accompanied me as far as the gate of the city, where I kissed her affectionately, which made me feel that the thunder and lightning had had but a momentary effect upon me; yet I kept control over my senses, and I congratulate myself on doing so to this day. I told her, before bidding her adieu, that, her virginity being no longer necessary for my magic operations, I advised her to get married as soon as possible, if I did not return within three months. She shed a few tears, but promised to follow my advice.

I trust that my readers will approve of the noble manner in which I concluded my magic business. I hardly dare to boast of it, but I think I deserve some praise for my behaviour. Perhaps, I might have ruined poor Franzia with a light heart, had I not possessed a well-filled purse. I do not wish to enquire whether any young man, having intelligence, loving pleasure, and placed in the same position, would not have done the same, but I beg my readers to address that question to themselves.

As for Capitani, to whom I sold the sheath of St. Peter's knife for rather more than it was worth, I confess that I have not yet repented on his account, for Capitani thought he had duped me in accepting it as security for the amount he gave me, and the count, his father, valued it until his death as more precious than the finest diamond in the world. Dying with such a firm belief, he died rich, and I shall die a poor man. Let the reader judge which of the two made the best bargain. But I must return now to my future travelling companions.

As soon as I had reached the inn, I prepared everything for our departure for which I was now longing. Henriette could not open her lips without my discovering some fresh perfection, for her wit delighted me even more than her beauty. It struck me that the old captain was pleased with all the attention I shewed her, and it seemed evident to me that she would not be sorry to exchange her elderly lover for me. I had all the better right to think so, inasmuch as I was perfection from a physical point of view, and I appeared to be wealthy, although I had no servant. I told Henriette that, for the sake of having none, I spent twice as much as a servant would have cost me, that, by my being my own servant, I was certain of being served according to my taste, and I had the satisfaction of having no spy at my heels and no privileged thief to fear. She agreed with everything I said, and it increased my love.

The honest Hungarian insisted upon giving me in advance the amount to be paid for the post-horses at the different stages as far as Parma. We left Cesena after dinner, but not without a contest of politeness respecting the seats. The captain wanted me to occupy the back seat-near Henriette, but the reader will understand how much better the seat opposite to her suited me; therefore I insisted upon taking the bracket-seat, and had the double advantage of shewing my politeness, and of having constantly and without difficulty before my eyes the lovely woman whom I adored.

My happiness would have been too great if there had been no drawback to it. But where can we find roses without thorns? When the charming Frenchwoman uttered some of those witty sayings which proceed so naturally from the lips of her countrywomen, I could not help pitying the sorry face of the poor Hungarian, and, wishing to make him share my mirth, I would undertake to translate in Latin Henriette's sallies; but far from making him merry, I often saw his face bear a look of astonishment, as if what I had said seemed to him rather flat. I had to acknowledge to myself that I could not speak Latin as well as she spoke French, and this was indeed the case. The last thing which we learn in all languages is wit, and wit never shines so well as in jests. I was thirty years of age before I began to laugh in reading Terence, Plautus and Martial.

Something being the matter with the carriage, we stopped at Forli to have it repaired. After a very cheerful supper, I retired to my room to go to bed, thinking of nothing else but the charming woman by whom I was so completely captivated. Along the road, Henriette had struck me as so strange that I would not sleep in the second bed in their room. I was afraid lest she should leave her old comrade to come to my bed and sleep with me, and I did not know how far the worthy captain would have put up with such a joke. I wished, of course, to possess that lovely creature, but I wanted everything to be settled amicably, for I felt some respect for the brave officer.

Henriette had nothing but the military costume in which she stood, not any woman's linen, not even one chemise. For a change she took the captain's shirt. Such a state of things was so new to me that the situation seemed to me a complete enigma.

In Bologna, excited by an excellent supper and by the amorous passion which was every hour burning more fiercely in me, I asked her by what singular adventure she had become the friend of the honest fellow who looked her father rather than her lover.

"If you wish to know," she answered, with a smile, "ask him to relate the whole story himself, only you must request him not to omit any of the particulars."

Of course I applied at once to the captain, and, having first ascertained by signs that the charming Frenchwoman had no objection, the good man spoke to me thus:

"A friend of mine, an officer in the army, having occasion to go to Rome, I solicited a furlough of six months, and accompanied him. I seized with great delight the opportunity of visiting a city, the name of which has a powerful influence on the imagination, owing to the memories of the past attached to it. I did not entertain any doubt that the Latin language was spoken there in good society, at least as generally as in Hungary. But I was indeed greatly mistaken, for nobody can speak it, not even the priests, who only pretend to write it, and it is true that some of them do so with great purity. I was therefore rather uncomfortable during my stay in Rome, and with the exception of my eyes my senses remained perfectly inactive. I had spent a very tedious month in that city, the ancient queen of the world, when Cardinal Albani gave my friend dispatches for Naples. Before leaving Rome, he introduced me to his eminence, and his recommendation had so much influence that the cardinal promised to send me very soon with dispatches for the Duke of Parma, Piacenza, and Guastalla, assuring me that all my travelling expenses would be defrayed. As I wished to see the harbour called in former times Centum cellae and now Civita-Vecchia, I gave up the remainder of my time to that visit, and I proceeded there with a cicerone who spoke Latin.

"I was loitering about the harbour when I saw, coming out of a tartan, an elderly officer and this young woman dressed as she is now. Her beauty struck me, but I should not have thought any more about it, if the officer had not put up at my inn, and in an apartment over which I had a complete view whenever I opened my window. In the evening I saw the couple taking supper at the same table, but I remarked that the elderly officer never addressed a word to the young one. When the supper was over, the disguised girl left the room, and her companion did not lift his eyes from a letter which he was reading, as it seemed to me, with the deepest attention. Soon afterwards the officer closed the windows, the light was put out, and I suppose my neighbors went to bed. The next morning, being up early as is my habit, I saw the officer go out, and the girl remained alone in the room.

"I sent my cicerone, who was also my servant, to tell the girl in the garb of an officer that I would give her ten sequins for an hour's conversation. He fulfilled my instructions, and on his return he informed me that her answer, given in French, had been to the effect that she would leave for Rome immediately after breakfast, and that, once in that city, I should easily find some opportunity of speaking to her.

"'I can find out from the vetturino,' said my cicerone, 'where they put up in Rome, and I promise you to enquire of him.'

"She left Civita-Vecchia with the elderly officer, and I returned home on the following day.

"Two days afterwards, the cardinal gave me the dispatches, which were addressed to M. Dutillot, the French minister, with a passport and the money necessary for the journey. He told me, with great kindness, that I need not hurry on the road.

"I had almost forgotten the handsome adventuress, when, two days before my departure, my cicerone gave me the information that he had found out where she lived, and that she was with the same officer. I told him to try to see her, and to let her know that my departure was fixed for the day after the morrow. She sent me word by him that, if I would inform her of the hour of my departure, she would meet me outside of the gate, and get into the coach with me to accompany me on my way. I thought the arrangement very ingenious and during the day I sent the cicerone to tell her the hour at which I intended to leave, and where I would wait for her outside of the Porto del Popolo. She came at the appointed time, and we have remained together ever since. As soon as she was seated near me, she made me understand by signs that she wanted to dine with me. You may imagine what difficulty we had in understanding one another, but we guessed somehow the meaning expressed by our pantomime, and I accepted the adventure with delight.

"We dined gaily together, speaking without understanding, but after the dessert we comprehended each other very well. I fancied that I had seen the end of it, and you may imagine how surprised I was when, upon my offering her the ten sequins, she refused most positively to take any money, making me understand that she would rather go with me to Parma, because she had some business in that city, and did not want to return to Rome.

"The proposal was, after all, rather agreeable to me; I consented to her wishes. I only regretted my inability to make her understand that, if she was followed by anyone from Rome, and if that person wanted to take her back, I was not in a position to defend her against violence. I was also sorry that, with our mutual ignorance of the language spoken by each of us, we had no opportunity of conversation, for I should have been greatly pleased to hear her adventures, which, I think, must be interesting. You can, of course, guess that I have no idea of who she can be. I only know that she calls herself Henriette, that she must be a Frenchwoman, that she is as gentle as a turtledove, that she has evidently received a good education, and that she enjoys good health. She is witty and courageous, as we have both seen, I in Rome and you in Cesena at General Spada's table. If she would tell you her history, and allow you to translate it for me in Latin she would indeed please me much, for I am sincerely her friend, and I can assure you that it will grieve me to part from her in Parma. Please to tell her that I intend to give her the thirty sequins I received from the

Bishop of Cesena, and that if I were rich I would give her more substantial proofs of my tender affection. Now, sir, I shall feel obliged to you if you will explain it all to her in French."

I asked her whether she would feel offended if I gave her an exact translation. She assured me that, on the contrary, she wished me to speak openly, and I told her literally what the captain had related to me.

With a noble frankness which a slight shade of-shame rendered more interesting, Henriette confirmed the truth of her friend's narrative, but she begged me to tell him that she could not grant his wish respecting the adventures of her life.

"Be good enough to inform him," she added, "that the same principle which forbids me to utter a falsehood, does not allow me to tell the truth. As for the thirty sequins which he intends to give me, I will not accept even one of them, and he would deeply grieve me by pressing them upon me. The moment we reach Parma I wish him to allow me to lodge wherever I may please, to make no enquiries whatever about me, and, in case he should happen to meet me, to crown his great kindness to me by not appearing to have ever known me."

As she uttered the last words of this short speech, which she had delivered very seriously and with a mixture of modesty and resolution, she kissed her elderly friend in a manner which indicated esteem and gratitude rather than love. The captain, who did not know why she was kissing him, was deeply grieved when I translated what Henriette had said. He begged me to tell her that, if he was to obey her with an easy conscience, he must know whether she would have everything she required in Parma.

"You can assure him," she answered, "that he need not entertain any anxiety about me."

This conversation had made us all very sad; we remained for a long time thoughtful and silent, until, feeling the situation to be painful, I rose, wishing them good night, and I saw that Henriette's face wore a look of great excitement.

As soon as I found myself alone in my room, deeply moved by conflicting feelings of love, surprise, and uncertainty, I began to give vent to my feelings in a kind of soliloquy, as I always do when I am strongly excited by anything; thinking is not, in those cases, enough for me; I must speak aloud, and I throw so much action, so much animation into these monologues that I forget I am alone. What I knew now of Henriette had upset me altogether.

"Who can she be," I said, speaking to the walls; "this girl who seems to have the most elevated feelings under the veil of the most cynical libertinism? She says that in Parma she wishes to remain perfectly unknown, her own mistress, and I cannot, of course, flatter myself that she will not place me under the same restrictions as the captain to whom she has already abandoned herself. Goodbye to my expectations, to my money, and my illusions! But who is she—what is she? She must have either a lover or a husband in Parma, or she must belong to a respectable family; or, perhaps, thanks to a boundless love for debauchery and to her confidence in her own charms, she intends to set fortune, misery, and degradation at defiance, and to try to enslave some wealthy nobleman! But that would be the plan of a mad woman or of a person reduced to utter despair, and it does not seem to be the case with Henriette. Yet she possesses nothing. True, but she refused, as if she had been provided with all she needed, the kind assistance of a man who has the right to offer it, and from whom, in sooth, she can accept without blushing, since she has not been ashamed to grant him favours with which love had nothing to do. Does she think that it is less shameful for a woman to abandon herself to the desires of a man unknown and unloved than to receive a present from an esteemed friend, and particularly at the eve of finding herself in the street, entirely destitute in the middle of a foreign city, amongst people whose language she cannot even speak? Perhaps she thinks that such conduct will justify the 'faux pas' of which she has been guilty with the captain, and give him to understand that she had abandoned herself to him only for the sake of escaping from the officer with whom she was in Rome. But she ought to be quite certain that the captain does not entertain any other idea; he shews himself so reasonable that it is impossible to suppose that he ever admitted the possibility of having inspired her with a violent passion, because she had seen him once through a window in Civita-Vecchia. She might possibly be right, and feel herself justified in her conduct towards the captain, but it is not the same with me, for with her intelligence she must be aware that I would not have travelled with them if she had been indifferent to me, and she must know that there is but one way in which she can obtain my pardon. She may be endowed with many virtues, but she has not the only one which could prevent me from wishing the reward which every man expects to receive at the hands of the woman he loves. If she wants to assume prudish manners towards me and to make a dupe of me, I am bound in honour to shew her how much she is mistaken."

After this monologue, which had made me still more angry, I made up my mind to have an explanation in the morning before our departure.

"I shall ask her," said I to myself, "to grant me the same favours which she has so easily granted to her old captain, and if I meet with a refusal the best revenge will be to shew her a cold and profound contempt until our arrival in Parma."

I felt sure that she could not refuse me some marks of real or of pretended affection, unless she wished to make a show of a modesty which certainly did not belong to her, and, knowing that her modesty would only be all pretence, I was determined not to be a mere toy in her hands.

As for the captain, I felt certain, from what he had told me, that he would not be angry with me if I risked a declaration, for as a sensible man he could only assume a neutral position.

Satisfied with my wise reasoning, and with my mind fully made up, I fell asleep. My thoughts were too completely absorbed by Henriette for her not to haunt my dreams, but the dream which I had throughout the night was so much like reality that, on awaking, I looked for her in my bed, and my imagination was so deeply struck with the delights of that night that, if my door had not been fastened with a bolt, I should have believed that she had left me during my sleep to resume her place near the worthy Hungarian.

When I was awake I found that the happy dream of the night had turned my love for the lovely creature into a perfect amorous frenzy, and it could not be other wise. Let the reader imagine a poor devil going to bed broken down with fatigue and starvation; he succumbs to sleep, that most imperative of all human wants, but in his dream he finds himself before a table covered with every delicacy; what will then happen? Why, a very natural result. His appetite, much more lively than on the previous day, does not give him a minute's rest he must satisfy it or die of sheer hunger.

I dressed myself, resolved on making sure of the possession of the woman who had inflamed all my senses, even before resuming our journey.

"If I do not succeed," I said to myself, "I will not go one step further."

But, in order not to offend against propriety, and not to deserve the reproaches of an honest man, I felt that it was my duty to have an explanation with the captain in the first place.

I fancy that I hear one of those sensible, calm, passionless readers, who have had the advantage of what is called a youth without storms, or one of those whom old age has forced to become virtuous, exclaim,

"Can anyone attach so much importance to such nonsense?"

Age has calmed my passions down by rendering them powerless, but my heart has not grown old, and my memory has kept all the freshness of youth; and far from considering that sort of thing a mere trifle, my only sorrow, dear reader, arises from the fact that I have not the power to practise, to the day of my death, that which has been the principal affair of my life!

When I was ready I repaired to the chamber occupied by my two travelling companions, and after paying each of them the usual morning compliments I told the officer that I was deeply in love with Henriette, and I asked him whether he would object to my trying to obtain her as my mistress.

"The reason for which she begs you," I added, "to leave her in Parma and not to take any further notice of her, must be that she hopes to meet some lover of hers there. Let me have half an hour's conversation with her, and I flatter myself I can persuade her to sacrifice that lover for me. If she refuses me, I remain here; you will go with her to Parma, where you will leave my carriage at the post, only sending me a receipt, so that I can claim it whenever I please."

"As soon as breakfast is over," said the excellent man, "I shall go and visit the institute, and leave you alone with Henriette. I hope you may succeed, for I should be delighted to see her under your protection when I part with her. Should she persist in her first resolution, I could easily find a 'vetturino' here, and you could keep your carriage. I thank you for your proposal, and it will grieve me to leave you."

Highly pleased at having accomplished half of my task, and at seeing myself near the denouement, I asked the lovely Frenchwoman whether she would like to see the sights of Bologna.

"I should like it very much," she said, "if I had some other clothes; but with such a costume as this I do not care to shew myself about the city."

"Then you do not want to go out?"

"No."

"Can I keep you company?"

"That would be delightful."

The captain went out immediately after breakfast. The moment he had gone I told Henriette that her friend had left us alone purposely, so as to give me the opportunity of a private interview with her.

"Tell me now whether you intended the order which you gave him yesterday to forget you, never to enquire after you; and even not to know you if he happened to meet you, from the time of our arrival in Parma, for me as well as for him."

"It is not an order that I gave him; I have no right to do so, and I could not so far forget myself; it is only a prayer I addressed to him, a service which circumstances have compelled me to claim at his hands, and as he has no right to refuse me, I never entertained any doubt of his granting my command. As far as you are concerned, it is certain that I should have addressed the same prayer to you, if I had thought that you had any views about me. You have given me some marks of your friendship, but you must understand that if, under the circumstances, I am likely to be injured by the kind attentions of the captain, yours would injure me much more. If you have any friendship for me, you would have felt all that."

"As you know that I entertain great friendship for you, you cannot possibly suppose that I would leave you alone, without money, without resources in the middle of a city where you cannot even make yourself understood. Do you think that a man who feels for you the most tender affection can abandon you when he has been fortunate enough to make your acquaintance, when he is aware of the sad position in which you are placed? If you think such a thing possible, you must have a very false idea of friendship, and should such a man grant your request, he would only prove that he is not your friend."

"I am certain that the captain is my friend; yet you have heard him, he will obey me, and forget me."

"I do not know what sort of affection that honest man feels for you, or how far he can rely upon the control he may have over himself, but I know that if he can grant you what you have asked from him, his friendship must be of a nature very different from mine, for I am bound to tell you it is not only impossible for me to afford you willingly the strange gratification of abandoning you in your position, but even that, if I go to Parma, you could not possibly carry out your wishes, because I love you so passionately that you must promise to be mine, or I must remain here. In that case you must go to Parma alone with the captain, for I feel that, if I accompanied you any further, I should soon be the most wretched of men. I could not bear to see you with another lover, with a husband, not even in the midst of your family; in fact, I would fain see you and live with you forever. Let me tell you, lovely Henriette, that if it is possible for a Frenchman to forget, an Italian cannot do it, at least if I judge from my own feelings. I have made up my mind, you must be good enough to decide now, and to tell me whether I am to accompany you or to remain here. Answer yes or no; if I remain here it is all over. I shall leave for Naples to-morrow, and I know I shall be cured in time of the mad passion I feel for you, but if you tell me that I can accompany you to Parma, you must promise me that your heart will forever belong to me alone. I must be the only one to possess you, but I am ready to accept as a condition, if you like, that you shall not crown my happiness until you have judged me worthy of it by my attentions and by my loving care. Now, be kind enough to decide before the return of the too happy captain. He knows all, for I have told him what I feel."

"And what did he answer?"

"That he would be happy to see you under my protection. But what is the meaning of that smile playing on your lips?"

"Pray, allow me to laugh, for I have never in my life realized the idea of a furious declaration of love. Do you understand what it is to say to a woman in a declaration which ought to be passionate, but at the same time tender and gentle, the following terrible words:

"'Madam, make your choice, either one or the other, and decide instanter!' Ha! ha! ha!"

"Yes, I understand perfectly. It is neither gentle, nor gallant, nor pathetic, but it is passionate. Remember that this is a serious matter, and that I have never yet found myself so much pressed by time. Can you, on your side, realize the painful position of a man, who, being deeply in love, finds himself compelled to take a decision which may perhaps decide issues of life and death? Be good enough to remark that, in spite of the passion raging in me, I do not fail in the respect I owe you; that the resolution I intend to take, if you should persist in your original decision, is not a threat, but an effort worthy of a hero, which ought to call for your esteem. I beg of you to consider that we cannot afford to lose time. The word choose must not sound harshly in your ears, since it leaves my fate as well as yours entirely in your hands. To feel certain of my love, do you want to see me kneeling before you like a simpleton, crying and entreating you to take pity on me? No, madam, that would certainly displease you, and it would not help me. I am conscious of being worthy of your love, I therefore ask for that feeling and not for pity. Leave me, if I displease you, but let me go away; for if you are humane enough to wish that I should forget you, allow me to go far away from you so as to make my sorrow less immense. Should I follow you to Parma, I would not answer for myself, for I might give way to my despair. Consider everything well, I beseech you; you would indeed be guilty of great cruelty, were you to answer now: 'Come to Parma, although I must beg of you not to see me in that city.' Confess that you cannot, in all fairness, give me such an answer; am I not right?"

"Certainly, if you truly love me."

"Good God! if I love you? Oh, yes! believe me, my love is immense, sincere! Now, decide my fate."

"What! always the same song?"

"Yes."

"But are you aware that you look very angry?"

"No, for it is not so. I am only in a state of uncontrollable excitement, in one of the decisive hours of my life, a prey to the most fearful anxiety. I ought to curse my whimsical destiny and the 'sbirri' of Cesena (may God curse them, too!), for, without them, I should never have known you."

"Are you, then, so very sorry to have made my acquaintance?"

"Have I not some reason to be so?"

"No, for I have not given you my decision yet."

"Now I breathe more freely, for I am sure you will tell me to accompany you to Parma."

"Yes, come to Parma."

The End